Biography

Alistair Edwards' interest in computers and in the needs of disabled people began when he was at the University of Warwick. There he gained a degree in Physics and Computer Science but at the same time became involved in voluntary work with children with disabilities. He continued to pursue both interests after graduation, working full time in a children's home for nine months, before going to the United States, to study for an MSc in Computer Science at Pennsylvania State University.

On returning to Britain he took on a job at the University of Manchester, Institute of Science and Technology, developing software programming tools. From there he went on to combine his two interests again by researching for a Doctorate in Educational Technology, in Special Education. This was at the Open University, where he had the opportunity to follow on work which had been done there on making computers accessible to blind people.

After having completed his PhD and lectured for a short time at the Open University, he moved on to join the Human–Computer Interaction Research Group at the University of York. He lectures in Computer Science and his main research interest continues to be how to make computers accessible to visually disabled people, mainly through the use of sounds – both speech and non-speech, as well as the more broad implications of multi-modal interfaces.

SPEECH SYNTHESIS

Series in Human Computer Interaction
Editor: Tim O'Shea

SPEECH SYNTHESIS
Technology for Disabled People

Alistair D. N. Edwards

P·C·P

Paul Chapman
Publishing Ltd

To my parents,
Norman and Beth Edwards

Copyright © 1991 Alistair D.N. Edwards

First published 1991
Paul Chapman Publishing Ltd
144 Liverpool Road
London
N1 1LA

Distributed exclusively in North America by
Paul H. Brookes Publishing Co. Inc.,
P.O. Box 10624
Baltimore
Maryland, 21285-0624

British Library Cataloguing in Publication Data
Edwards, Alistair D. N.
  Speech synthesis for disabled people.
  1. Speech. Synthesis. Applications of computer systems
  I. Title
  006.54

  ISBN 1-85396-066-7

Typeset by DP Photosetting, Aylesbury, Bucks
Printed and bound by Butler & Tanner, Frome, Somerset

A B C D E F G   5 4 3 2 1

Contents

Foreword

Alistair Edwards is a talented young computer scientist who arrived a few years ago at the Open University announcing his wish to do anything with computers as long as it was socially useful. He selected as his research target a contemporary set back for blind computer users. Blind people who used speech synthesizers attached to computer terminals or microcomputers suddenly found themselves excluded from the use of a new generation of software which laid out material visually on computer screens using 'windows' and 'icons' controlled by hand held pointing devices such as 'mice'. In the research for his doctorate he broke new ground when he designed, implemented and evaluated software which used sounds (as well as speech) to guide blind users from window to window.

Alistair has now established himself as a specialist in human computer interaction who combines a thorough mastery of the scientific and technological issues with a commitment to the needs of computer users with special needs. This book presents a thorough review of the state of the art in speech synthesis and focuses on the utility of this technology for blind computer users and for people who cannot speak. This book is clear and accurate when it describes technology but the discussion is always underpinned by clear statements on the value of the technology and the evidence from field trials or psychological testing on how the technology works.

There are three sound reasons for reading this book. First, it provides a thorough account, with appropriate history and pictures, of what speech synthesis is and how it works. Secondly, the case studies in the book provide a series of heartening examples of socially beneficial uses of computer technology. Finally, this is an honest and very well written book. No attempt is made to 'talk up' any particular technological development and Alistair has managed to produce a book on human computer interaction which is an enjoyable and engaging read.

Tim O'Shea
Series Editor
1990

Preface

'Disability'

Two characteristics distinguish humans from other species: technology and language. There may be others, such as the possession of a soul, but such religious and philosophical concepts are far beyond the scope of this book, whereas technology and language are its very subject matter. Living in a largely hostile environment, the human body has many severe limitations: it cannot run very fast, it cannot fly, it is badly equipped to fight, it does not even have sufficient hair to keep itself warm enough in most climates. Yet people have devised and built technologies which have overcome all of these – and other – shortcomings. In a sense, what humans lack in terms of physical abilities, they have compensated for by application of their developed mental ability (though in the development of technology the importance of having a hand which works so efficiently should not be overlooked). Each individual has a different set of abilities, but for the most part we are essentially similar. There are those, however, whose capabilities are limited to the extent that their ability to function in society is restricted – to the extent that they are classed as being 'disabled'.

One approach to disability is to extend the idea of adapting the environment to the person, outlined above; to extend the technology to meet the special needs of individuals. That is the subject matter of this book. Usually the effect of disability is to make a person more dependent on other people. (In a society we are all dependent on others to some extent.) However, *independence* is a much valued quality, and it is therefore very desirable that people should have the chance of living with maximum independence, which can often be achieved through appropriate application of technology.

Terms like 'disability' and 'disabled' are awkward and often misused. Not the least, they can be used in such a way that they imply there are two kinds of people: 'the disabled' and 'the normal'. Such labels are inappropriate and can be quite harmful. In the light of the above discussion, it might be said that an appropriate use of the term 'disabled' is to imply that the subject has significant restrictions on his or her independence.

This book is concerned with the use of a specific technology, mainly by two different groups: people who cannot speak and blind people who use computers. I admit that the book's title implies that I am grouping these two disparate groups together under the banner, but such is the nature of book titles; they have to catch the eye of people who have an interest in their subject. Would you have picked this book up if it had been entitled *Speech Synthesis and Its Use by People with Restricted Independence?* The common subject matter is speech synthesis. The needs of the different users are diverse, but their use of the technology is sufficiently similar to be contained in the same book.

On the basis of that discussion, I hope readers will forgive me for any negative associations that the book's title may have for them. It is often said that emphasis should be placed on people's abilities – what they can do, rather than what they cannot. This book is about what people can do, with a little help from the technology.

Acknowledgements

A great big thanks and hug are due to Kathy McLaughlin for her practical help in reading and commenting on an early draft of this book, as well as her moral and practical support during its writing.

Some of the work described in this book was supervised by Tim O'Shea, whose idea it was to write the book in the first place. He has been a source of invaluable inspiration and support over several years, for which I will always be grateful.

Tom Vincent was a major influence on my moving into this area of work and he has also been very helpful with supplying information for use in this book. Peter Bailey, Ian Pitt, Janet Finlay and Caitriona McHugh kindly took the time to read draft chapters and provided a number of extremely useful comments.

Charles Court kindly demonstrated his use of Outspoken and Andrew Miles of the Billingham Employment Rehabilitation Centre demonstrated the Kurzweil Personal Reader. This was arranged with the help of Melvin Robinson of Sight & Sound Technology. Further detailed information was supplied by Anita Hunt of Eric Leach Marketing Ltd.

Information on Minspeak was supplied by Katie Sutton of Liberator Ltd and Tony Jones of Portland Training Centre kindly supplied a full description of the Language, Learning and Living Map.

Tony Vitale of Digital Electronic Corporation in Massachusetts took the trouble to reply by telephone to a speculative inquiry letter and gave much useful information on Dectalk.

David Calderwood and Stephen Hawking provided help and inspiration.

John Tillisch of Sensory Systems Ltd supplied information and advice on the Frank Audiodata.

Andy Lowe of the Centre for Speech Technology Research at Edinburgh University kindly provided the spectrogram (Figure 2.2).

The book was written entirely on an Apple Macintosh computer. Thanks must be given to the Management Committee of the Institute of Educational Technology at the Open University, who loaned me a hard disc beyond the end of my appointment there, enabling me to continue work on the book. The hard disc was of use to me only thanks to the loan of a computer, this time from Geoff Crumplin of the Biology Department at York University.

Tea-time with the Brat Pack was responsible for a great deal of inspiration, some of which has found its way into this book.

Finally, I must mention my parents, who have supported me in so many ways through the years. From them I have inherited the enjoyment of writing – and been taught the importance of grammar and spelling. In particular my father, Norman Edwards, took the time to read a complete draft and provided invaluable assistance with improvements in style.

Trademarks

Many of the designations used by manufacturers and sellers to distinguish their products are claimed as trademarks. The author and publishers have made every attempt to supply trademark information about manufacturers and their products mentioned in this book.

Apple, Macintosh, SonicFinder are registered trademarks of Apple Computer Inc.

MS-DOS is a registered trademark of Microsoft Corporation.

Personal System/2 is a trademark of International Business Machines Corp.

Echo PC is a trademark of Street Electronics Corp.

Light Talker and Touch Talker are registered trademarks of the Prentke Romich Company.

MicroVax is a registered trademark of Digital Equipment Corporation.

Votrax and Type'n' Talk are trademarks of Votrax Inc.

1　Introduction

Using Machines which Speak

Speech is the most important form of human communication. Its use is unique to people. People have long been fascinated by the possibility of investing inanimate machines with the power of speech – or at least something resembling it. Since the invention of the gramophone it has been possible to store and recreate speech, but it is only quite recently that has been possible to generate novel (reasonably) intelligible speech. Reactions to talking computers vary. Some people feel rather as Dr Johnson did regarding dogs which can walk on their hind legs, 'It is not done well; but you are surprised to find it done at all', while others take a rather more practical view that the quality of the speech is generally so unnatural that it is a disappointment. Hopefully, Chapter 2 will reconcile these two viewpoints by convincing the reader that reproducing human-like speech is a very difficult enterprise, that a great deal of progress has been made towards achieving it and that we can only expect it to get better within the next few years.

Now that the technology to generate synthetic speech is available, people are searching around for applications in which it should be used. Some are little more than gimmicks, such as the car which talks to the driver, saying when his or her seat belt is not fastened, for instance. Researchers and designers are still investigating the principles which ought to be applied to decide when it is appropriate to use synthetic speech as a means of communication. For example, an aircraft flight-deck is an environment very similar to a car driver's seat, and in that case it has been found to be appropriate to use synthetic speech to communicate warnings to the pilots, giving them precise information regarding the state of the aircraft without distracting their vision from their instruments.

One area in which speech synthesis has an obvious application, however, is in the area of providing assistance to people with disabilities – and that is the subject of this book.

It should be emphasized that this book is concerned with machines which speak to people. People speaking to (and being 'understood' by) machines is a completely different field. Although such speech recognition has its application for use by some disabled people the technology is very different. Readers who have an interest in the possibilities might consult Poulton (1983).

This book is aimed at a very broad audience. The reader is not expected to have any technical background. Jargon is avoided as much as possible, but where it has had to be used there is a glossary available. (Terms appearing in the glossary are printed in bold type on the first occasion they are used in each chapter.) Chapter 2 is the most technical. It presents quite a brief introduction to speech technology. It will be of interest to those with some technical background but who have not come across speech synthesis technology as such. On the other hand, readers with less of an interest in how a speech synthesizer generates its sounds may prefer to skim or skip that chapter, and should be able to do so without affecting their understanding of the rest of the book.

In writing about the liberating power of technology, it is tempting to single out celebrated instances of its use. Professor Stephen Hawking is thought by many to be the greatest living physicist. There is little doubt that, due to his having motor neurone disease, he would probably not still be working were it not for the the availability of speech synthesizers. At the same time one must not belittle the significance of the technology to other, less well-known people. To be able to communicate with one's family may be just as important as being able to give lectures to groups of eminent scientists.

Who Needs Speech Prostheses?

Synthetic speech is useful in different ways to two groups of people who are described as disabled. There are people who lack the physical ability to produce speech. For them, synthetic speech can become their voice via a speech-based communicator. They will be referred to as 'expressive' synthetic speech users. The other group who can benefit from synthetic speech are blind people, who use it as a means of receiving information which might otherwise be presented in a written form. In particular it is a means of access to computer output. It is stressed that the requirements of synthetic speech for these two groups of people are very different. It is the common technology which they use that unites them in this context.

It is important to make some definitions and clarifications regarding disability before getting into any further discussions. The Preface includes a definition of disability in general terms, but it is useful to be more specific at this point. It is accepted that people have wide-ranging levels of achievement and potential in their mental and physical faculties. By definition, the level at which the majority function is considered to be average – or normal. Of course, many people are exceptional; they have an ability which is not average. Often such exceptions are evident only in one or two faculties in an individual. So, for instance, a successful athlete is abnormal in his or her physical powers (i.e abnormally well provided). A painter has better artistic abilities – but probably could not run any faster than average. Indeed, the painter may be a slower runner than his or her contemporaries, but since running is not a vital skill in most people's lives, the painter's lack is not a serious one. However, if people have impairments which seriously affect their capacity to take a full part in society, they are said to be disabled.[1]

---

[1] The terms 'disability' and 'handicap' are often confused. 'Handicap' refers to the effect that a person's disability has on his or her life.

The line which divides those who are said to be disabled from those who are not is a blurred one. Someone who cannot see at all is clearly at a disadvantage in the visually orientated world, and can be said to be disabled. However, among the population who can see, visual acuity is not at all uniform. In any group of people, some will see better than others. A few will have sight significantly less acute than the majority, but will still be able to lead a similar life. Yet at some point, a person's sight – while it does exist – is so ineffective that he or she is said to be disabled. In fact the great majority of people who have a visual disability are not blind, but *partially sighted*. This lack of clear definition is a feature common to all forms of disability. It would be very convenient if it was possible to divide the population into 'the sighted' and 'the blind' or 'the normal' and 'the disabled' (and indeed some people try to do that), but to so do is to commit a gross and damaging oversimplification. Using adjectives as nouns, such as 'the disabled', is to be avoided since it is dehumanizing and often implies a wholly inappropriate generalization.

'Visual disability' is a generic term, taken to cover both partial sight and blindness. 'Blindness' is used quite specifically in this book. The needs of partially sighted people are very different from those of blind people and are not generally addressed by the use of speech synthesis. Partially sighted people generally need to make maximum use of their residual vision. Any aids they might use should therefore be designed to boost the power of their residual sight. The simple example is the use of magnification to enhance poor vision. By contrast, a blind person has no sight and therefore needs to use another sense instead. For example, access to printed text can be achieved by converting it to a tactile form, such as braille, or an auditory form – such as synthetic speech.

Another factor which makes it difficult and inappropriate to apply labels to individuals or groups of people with disabilities is the fact that people often have serious impairments of more than one faculty. For instance, a person may have had a brain injury which affects ability to speak, but it may also result in insufficient manual control to use a typewriter keyboard.

Speech is a unique form of communication. Hence synthetic speech is an important alternative for people who cannot speak naturally. As far as expressive users of synthetic speech are concerned, this book reviews how near the technology has come to providing them with facilities analogous to those of natural speech – and how far there is still to go.

For blind people the attractions of synthetic speech are simpler. A visual impairment does not affect a person's comprehension of speech, so its use requires no special training. In most of the computer adaptations which are studied here, the essential need is to convert visual text output by computers into an auditory form, although in Chapter 5 we examine the adaptation of computers where speech alone is not enough.

Expressive Communication

Whereas blind people using speech as a means of receiving information from computers are referred to as 'receptive' users, this section introduces those who use it as a means of communicating to other people, who will be called 'expressive' users.

A number of different conditions can make it impossible for an individual to speak naturally. These can be grouped under three broad headings: damage to the speech-production mechanisms, lack of sufficient muscular control and cognitive impairment. These headings are *not* distinct. For instance, a lack of muscular control may be due to cognitive factors. Also, it is quite common for people to have more than one form of disability, which may mean that as well as not being able to speak they are limited in their access to communications devices.

Damage to the speech-production mechanisms may be caused by illness, such as infections or abnormal growths. It may also occur as a result of physical trauma, as all too commonly occurs in road traffic accidents. Injury may also accidentally occur during medical treatment, such as when tubes are inserted into the windpipe during anaesthesia, or when a endoscope is inserted down the throat as a means of examining the stomach.

Growths on the vocal cords (vocal folds) may be benign or malignant. Such illnesses may have to be treated by surgery. The vocal cords may have to be removed – a total laryngectomy – often as a means of maintaining respiration and swallowing, but at the cost of the voice. Another surgical procedure is a tracheostomy, whereby the vocal tract is by-passed through a hole in the throat.

Speech involves not just the vocal cords but also other organs, often with more than one role. For instance, it is necessary to be able to create a flow of air – using the organs primarily concerned with respiration. Speech is therefore also vulnerable to damage to these organs, such as infection of the upper respiratory tract.

In some cases the vocal cords may apparently not be damaged when at rest, but display abnormal movement. This may be due to damage to the central nervous system, which can be caused by illnesses including multiple sclerosis, Parkinson's disease, motor neurone disease and the effects of strokes. These conditions are significant in that they affect not only speech but also other physical functions. As is discussed much more later, this can be a very important factor in the design of communication aids which often must be usable by people with (for instance) very limited manual dexterity.

Vocal communication has two components: language and speech. Linguists disagree as to the extent that one is dependent on the other, but it is easy to demonstrate that the two are to some extent separable. For instance, someone may not be able to speak in that he or she cannot produce the sounds of speech because of a physical impairment (such as a total laryngectomy). However, he or she may be able to communicate through another medium such as sign language, so demonstrating a clearly unimpaired language ability.

It is very difficult to assess the intellectual ability of a person who cannot speak. It is only through expression that a person's intelligence can be assessed by another. The inability to speak obviously inhibits communication and probably retards development of other forms of expression. At the same time a great deal of what we consider to be intelligence is bound up with communication and language. It is all too common for those with one obvious form of disability to be treated by other people as if they are globally impaired. Thus, a blind person is shouted at, as if he or she must also be deaf, and most people with disabilities can recount stories of being treated as if they were a child or an idiot. This is so much worse for a person who cannot speak and is therefore more likely to be perceived as unintelligent, while at the same time is probably unable to disabuse the other person. It is important to emphasize that the speech comprehension of most users of communication aids is not impaired.

One alternative to using synthetic speech in a communication aid is to use printed output of some form – either on paper or a visual display. The obvious advantage of speech is that it is most like the form of communication it is replacing. As is the case for receptive users, the accessibility of speech is a major point in its favour. Unlike specialist forms of communication, such as sign language, it is understandable by the vast majority of the population. It also requires less attention on the part of the listener; the recipient of communication from a print-based device must look at the printed output. The recipient must also be able to read, which precludes communication with people who are illiterate, and in particular young children. Having stated the advantages of speech-based devices, they do have their disadvantages, which will become apparent in the more general discussions below.

There are other low-technology alternative forms of communication, based on the use of word boards of one form or another. The word board essentially consists of a table of words and communication takes place by the 'speaker' pointing at words in turn which the 'listener' can read out. The manner of pointing may be simply through the finger, but for those who lack the dexterity to point in this way there are a variety of pointers and mechanical assistance they can apply. The words need not be written in plain text. The Blissymbolics system is an iconically based language consisting of symbols which represent concepts. Although Bliss users normally communicate by simple pointing at a board of symbols, there have been experiments into incorporating speech (reported in Carlson, Granström and Hunnicutt, 1982). The idea of synthetic speech communication based on a symbolic language has also been taken further in the development of Minspeak, which is discussed fully in Chapter 4.

This book concentrates on the technology. In some senses that is often the easiest aspect. The electronic components which generate synthetic speech may be complex, but they are at least predictable and governed by physical laws. Social aspects of the use of technology are much less predictable and tractable. Just giving someone a voice he or she would otherwise lack does not necessarily mean anyone will listen to that person – especially if that voice sounds odd and mechanical and takes a long time to be generated. The normal rules of conversation do not work and it will only be with practice and familiarity that users of synthetic speech communicators will be assimilated into social situations. Of course, development of the technology will help. The nearer the communication comes to natural speech (in quality of voice, speed of generation, etc.) the less effort will be required for that assimilation to take place.

Use of Synthetic Speech by Blind People

The greatest use of synthetic speech by blind people has been in the provision of consumer products such as clocks, watches and calculators. Tactile watches do exist, and many people prefer still to use these since they can be consulted more unobtrusively. An interesting phenomenon of these talking everyday gadgets is that they have generally not been designed specifically for blind people. Some sighted people find it useful to have the time spoken to them rather than having to look at a watch or clock. Manufacturers have tended to produce these devices with speech as a gimmick – which has the bonus of making them usable by blind people.

Although these consumer products are in quite widespread use their interaction with the user is quite simple and so is not considered further, except that a number of them are listed and described in Appendix A. More challenging is the use of speech to make complex computer interfaces accessible to blind people, and this is the main use of synthetic speech by blind people which will be considered.

Throughout the development of computer technology one aspect which has remained constant is that the output from the computer has always been overwhelmingly visual. This has obviously put users who are blind at a real disadvantage, yet they have the same need to use computers as everyone else, in work, education and leisure. For a long time, though, the output of computers was almost entirely printed text, usually displayed on a television-like screen. The advent of speech synthesizers made it possible to give blind people access to the text by converting it into speech. This may seem an obvious idea, but its successful application is not a simple case of plugging a speech synthesizer into a computer so that it speaks everything on the screen. There must be a means of controlling what is spoken.

Readers of printed text do not start at the top of the page and read forward to the end. They recap, re-read words or phrases, skip and skim. Thus, even if the user of a speech synthesizer wanted simply to read a textbook, having it spoken from start to finish would not be appropriate. He or she must have the ability to control the speech in a manner similar to the sighted reader. In fact, most computer use is much more interactive than that anyway; it is more likely that the user will be composing the text (on a **word processor**) than just listening to the writings of another author. Such use definitely demands a high degree of control over the speaking of the text on the screen.

One approach to providing blind people with spoken computer output is to build programs which are designed to 'display' their output as speech. This has the advantage that the **software** can be tailored to the needs of the potential users, and the output can be optimized for auditory presentation. A disadvantage is that it limits the range of **application** software accessible to blind people. It also means that each application has to be specially written.

The alternative approach is to build an adaptation which will make standard software accessible to blind users. This is the approach embodied by the *screen reader*. Screen readers are described in greater detail later, but their great attraction is that they allow blind users access to standard, visual software. The user runs an application (word processor, **database, spreadsheet** or whatever) which displays text on the screen but the user has access to that text through the screen reader. There is no need to develop special programs for blind users; blind and sighted people can use the same software. In principle the effort of adaptation needs to be expended only once; one screen reader will give access to (nearly) all applications. This gives blind people the same range of choice of applications as sighted users. There is a vast selection of application software on the market. Computer users often become very animated in discussing the merits of their favourite piece of software and it is only fair that blind users should have access to just as wide a range of software. There are other practical advantages in that blind workers will be using the same applications as their sighted colleagues, and can share data with them. There is also an important psychological aspect in that many disabled people prefer that any special concessions made for them should be minimal.

Word processing is the most common use of computers by blind people. However, they often use the word processor for purposes other than producing high-quality documents. For sighted people it is easier and quicker when making rough notes to use a pen and paper, but since this is not accessible to blind people, they may use some form of word processor for this kind of task too[1]. Some people use portable computers with screen readers for this kind of task, but there are also custom-made talking note-takers available (see Eureka and Braille 'n' Speak, in Appendix A).

Greater impetus has been given to the development of adaptations of computers for people with disabilities (including blindness), by the passing of legislation in the United States. The law means that manufacturers who wish to sell computers to the largest customer in the world (the US government) must pay regard to how they can be made accessible to disabled workers. This is explained further in the first section of Chapter 3.

Characteristics of Speech

Speech is a fundamental form of communication. This section briefly summarizes the fundamental characteristics of speech.

When meeting people for the first time we rapidly make judgements about them. It is important for us to decide quickly with what sort of person we are dealing. No doubt this is a primitive instinct. Our cave-dwelling ancestors probably had to decide quickly whether anyone they encountered was likely to club them over the head or challenge their territory. Nowadays the weapons may be less conspicuous, but the threats still exist. When you meet new people what is the first thing you notice about them? You probably look them over and take in their general appearance, the sort of clothes they are wearing and suchlike. Your second opinion is probably formed when they speak. Not only is what they say important, but also how they say it. You might notice the pleasantness – or otherwise – of the sound of their voice. Their accent will be important too – giving you an indication of how close their origins are to your own, both geographically and socially. Without having to apprehend the words they say, you will judge whether they are speaking confidently, or whether there is a hesitation in their speech, suggesting uncertainty.

Speech Is Universal

Anyone who cannot use speech is by definition handicapped. The loss of the power of speech is normally associated with some broader recognizable disability. Audible speech is not accessible to profoundly deaf people (though, of course, many such people learn to understand speech in its visual manifestation of lip movements) and cannot be produced by people with the sorts of disabilities mentioned earlier, in Who needs speech prostheses? Of course there are cultural limitations on the use of speech in that different languages are used, but the essentials of the speech medium remain constant. By contrast, a person who is illiterate is at a disadvantage in society, but is not classed as being disabled. Speech is so fundamental that children learn it with very little effort; no formal lessons are necessary to get a child to learn to use this powerful medium. Speech is also the medium of most conscious thought; we 'speak' silently to ourselves.

---

[1] Braille users do have the alternative of using various note-taking devices, ranging from braille 'typewriters' to small portable frames and styli which are used to emboss braille dots manually.

Rate of Speech Communication

Speech is produced very rapidly. Conversations normally proceed at a rate of around 150 words per minute. Though it is easy to measure the rate of communication in terms of words per minute, it is rather more difficult to compare it in terms of information content.

Speech Is Extremely Expressive

The fact that human speech is extremely rich is well illustrated by the difficulty technologists have experienced in trying to imitate it, as described in Chapter 2. As will be explained more fully in that chapter, the characteristics of speech can be divided into two broad areas: *segmental* and *suprasegmental* features. Essentially, the segmental features are those which convey the basic information of the utterance, the words and their message. In other words, the segmental features embody the sounds of the words. The suprasegmental features convey information over and above the content of the words. These include prosody, and characteristics such as the quality of the voice. (See Chapter 2 for a further discussion of these aspects of speech.) Some of the suprasegmental features contribute to the sense that speech is very personal. The way a person speaks is an aspect of his or her character, affecting the way he or she is perceived by others and the way he or she would like to be perceived. These personal signals are embodied in aspects such as accent, voice quality and vocabulary.

Speech Is Slow

The sound signals of speech contain a high degree of redundancy, so that it is relatively slow but rich. The upper limit of the speed of speech is imposed more by production constraints than limits of comprehension. It is possible to understand tape recordings of speech played back at an increased speed. It is very common for blind people who rely on tape recordings as a replacement for written text (such as 'talking books') to use this technique as a means of increasing their rate of communication. Simply playing a tape at an increased speed does also lead to a rise in the pitch of the speech – a Mickey Mouse-like voice. However, some variable-speed tape players have the facility to correct the pitch to normal levels. With such equipment it is possible to listen to speech at speeds similar to that of a sighted person silently reading (i.e. around 500 words per minute).

Speaking Is a Physical Act

Speech cannot be separated from other physical forms of communication which generally accompany it in the form of body language. A conversation by telephone, whereby the body language is missing, is very different from a face-to-face interaction. However, speech does not require a great deal of physical effort; most people can spend a large proportion of their waking day engaged in speech.

Speech Is an Auditory Medium

It has a number of characteristics which are common to all sounds. Speech and other sounds are very transient in nature. The listener does not have the same opportunity to review information which is expressed in a written form. Memory limitations become significant. For instance, people generally speak in short sentences because it is quite possible to lose the thread of a sentence before it is complete, the listener forgetting how it started.

Speech does not require the full attention of the listener or listeners. They need not look anywhere in particular and use of the limbs is not necessary, so that a person can be doing other things at the same time as playing a full part in a conversation. A speaker can address a wide range of numbers of listeners, from whispering very specifically to one individual to addressing a large auditorium full of people. With the assistance of technology such as radio or recording, the audience for speech is effectively unlimited.

It is often assumed that hearing is essentially a *serial* medium. When viewing information visually it is very quick and easy to switch attention between different events. In fact, this switching is so fast that it is possible to observe several events occurring in parallel, but in receiving information aurally it seems that we do not have quite the same ability. Nevertheless it is undoubtedly true that people can receive a certain amount of parallel information aurally. For instance, a complex sound – such as an orchestra, or even speech – contains a vast amount of information in several forms at once (a set of tones and overtones, **amplitude**, rhythm, etc.) which we can receive and appreciate. Generally a listener can concentrate on only one source of complex auditory information, such as speech, at any time. However, there are phenomena such as the well-known 'cocktail party effect', whereby an individual may be engaged in a conversation at a party and apparently devoting all his or her attention to the speaker, yet will notice should someone say his or her name across the room at quite a low level. More research is required into how this latent ability can be exploited more in speech devices.

Human–Computer Interface Design

This book is concerned with interaction between people and computers, or at least particular people using computers which incorporate the use of synthetic speech. Where two components of a technological system are connected is often referred to as the 'interface'. This term has been extended to describe the techniques and technology of connecting people to computers: the human–computer interface.

The design of the human–computer interface is critical. Only if the computer is sufficiently easy and pleasant to use (by way of the interface) will it be used at all. That is true of all computer systems, which is why human–computer interaction has become such an important area of research and development. However, the interface has even greater significance for the users studied herein because they all have some disability which affects their ability to communicate. Highly specialized interfaces must be built for users who cannot see a screen or cannot type on a keyboard. Chapter 3 includes a fuller discussion of the implications of human–computer interface design, but it is also a theme which runs throughout the book.

Help! Where to Turn for Advice

The use of microelectronic technology to assist disabled people is a rapidly evolving field and it is very difficult to keep up with new trends and developments. It is also moving from being something pursued by enthusiasts in their spare time to a realistically commercial venture. These factors mean it can be hard for anyone to obtain good, unbiased advice.

In Britain the best place to turn to for assessments of the needs of individuals is the National Federation of Access Centres. This is a nationwide network of centres, based mostly in colleges of further education, with a rich experience of the use of computer-based devices by people with all kinds of disabilities. For a fee they will carry out a full assessment of an individual's needs and recommend the best available options. It must be said that they are not blinded by the heat of high technology, and are quite prepared to recommend traditional approaches if they are the best for the individual. Being a distributed network of centres, they can usually arrange that an assessment is carried out by someone reasonably local to the client. Assessments can be carried out in the client's home, though it is usually much better if the client can travel to the nearest centre, where a wide range of equipment is available for testing and comparison.

Another source of unbiased information in the UK is the Handicapped Persons' Research Unit. This is a centre dedicated to projects in research and design of aids for use by disabled people, and to the collection and dissemination of information on available products. The Unit has databases available on software, employment, non-medical research and microelectronic-based technology.

A source of advice for students and would-be students is Skill, the National Bureau for Students with Disabilities. Both the Royal National Institute for the Blind's Commercial Training College and the Royal National College for the Blind offer courses on the use of computers with speech output.

The Department of Health and the Royal Association for Disability and Rehabilitation (RADAR) have established a national network of Communication Aids Centres. Their addresses are given in Appendix B, under Communication Aids Centres. There is also a network of Disabled Living Centres which have permanent exhibitions of a wide range of equipment which clients can try out before they commit themselves to buying.

The institution which performs much the same function in the United States is the Trace Research and Development Center on Communication, Control and Computer Access for Handicapped Individuals. It also has large databases of information and a vast supply of reprints of papers and reports on equipment and adaptations.

The addresses of all the above-mentioned institutions can be found in Appendix B.

Layout of the Book

Chapter 2 is an introduction to the technology of speech synthesis. By first describing the mechanisms of human speech production, it gives a suggestion why it is so difficult to achieve good-quality synthetic speech. The speech synthesizer is just one component of the technology, and is useless unless people can interact with it. Thus Chapter 3 examines the design of the human–computer interface in the context of the particular computers and devices covered by this book.

The discussions of the earlier chapters are put into context in Chapter 4, which consists of a small set of case studies of commercially available devices. The products included are two speech communicators – with very different user interfaces – a machine which will read books out loud and a screen reader.

Chapter 5 looks more toward the future. It shows that with continuing development of computers speech alone is not sufficiently powerful to allow access to blind users. This chapter therefore describes work which has been carried out as a step in that direction.

The final chapter is also forward-looking. It describes some new devices which have not (yet) made it into commercial production, but which show some interesting innovations. It also goes even farther into the future in speculating as to what other developments may occur.

Within the text there are references to further reading in articles and books. A full list of the references will be found at the end of the book. Most chapters conclude with a section headed 'Further Reading', which contains pointers to wider reading related to the topic of the chapter which has not been specifically referenced in the body of the chapter.

Appendix A provides useful resources in that it lists available speech-based devices and their suppliers, and Appendix B lists addresses of organizations and of the manufacturers and suppliers of the equipment mentioned in Appendix A. Appendix C is a brief introduction to the physics of sound, which will be helpful in the reading of Chapter 3 for readers who do not have that basic background.

Further Reading

Carroll Center for the Blind (1983) is a somewhat dated journal, particularly in its reviews of available equipment. However, its papers on the requirements of speech-based systems are as valid as ever.

Edworthy and Patterson (1985) and Patterson (1982) present guidelines as to how speech should be used in aircraft warnings.

Fawcus (1986) includes a detailed though somewhat technical description of the sorts of disorders which can lead to a loss of the ability to speak.

Poulton (1983) provides a good general introduction to speech synthesis, but also covers speech recognition for any reader whose interest extends to that area.

Shearer (1981) examines disability and handicap in our society.

Teja (1981) is another readable introduction to speech synthesis.

2   Speech and Technology

Scope

This chapter will establish the framework within which the designer of a speech-based device must work. Natural speech can be seen as the ideal towards which speech synthesizer designers aspire, so natural speech production is explained. That is followed by a description of modern speech technology illuminating the design compromises the designers have to make. This will help to clarify the questions which potential users of speech technology might ask – and explanations of the answers they might receive. This is intended to be broad introduction to the technology, rather than a deep technical description of speech synthesis. For those interested in the mathematical and/or electronic details plenty of references are cited at the end of the chapter. Similarly, any reader who is not familiar with the basic physics of sound may wish to consult Appendix C.

Compromise in Design

Designing any product is a matter of compromise; there is no one ideal design for any product. So, the designer of a speech synthesizer, or any device which is going to use speech output, must weigh up the costs and benefits of each decision. The factors that such a designer would have to consider are:

- vocabulary requirement;
- monetary cost;
- intelligibility and naturalness of the speech output;
- speed of communication.

Some speaking devices need only a fixed vocabulary. For instance, a talking calculator will have a vocabulary of about twenty-four words, corresponding to one word per calculator key. Other devices must have an unlimited vocabulary, to be able to express normal conversation for instance. As will be shown later, the decision whether fixed or unlimited vocabulary will be used can have a significant influence on the type of synthesizer used and hence on the quality of the speech attainable. The importance of quality depends very much on the use being made of the speech, and particularly whether it is to be used for expressive or receptive communication. Quality is an important topic, and is considered fully in a later section of this chapter.

Another important consideration in any design is the cost of manufacture, and that is obviously largely dependent on the cost of the product's components. A major component of any information technology device is its **memory**. Basically, the more memory a device has the greater the cost, but it is not as simple as that. Another property of memory is its speed – how quickly an item can be retrieved. High-capacity memory is available at lower cost if a slower speed is acceptable. The main memory of a computer consists of memory chips, which are very fast, but comparatively expensive. Larger amounts of supporting memory are usually provided by a disc, which has much greater capacity but which is very much slower, being a mechanical device. (Discs also have the advantage of being *non-volatile* – they retain their information even when the power is switched off.) So, again, the designer is faced with making a compromise. Another important phenomenon in this context is the rapid development of memory **hardware**, which has the effect that it is constantly becoming cheaper. For the same amount of money that a developer might have spent last year it is now possible to buy memory of greater capacity and greater speed. So it must always be borne in mind that what is not now practical because of memory limitations, may become feasible within quite a short time.

Phonetics

Before discussing the mechanics of speech production it is necessary to establish a vocabulary and notation based on the science of phonetics. The basic building blocks of speech are *phonemes*. The phoneme is the smallest segment of sound such that if one phoneme in a word is substituted with another, the meaning may be changed. For example, substituting the first phoneme in 'coffee' could change the word to 'toffee'.

Because the definition is somewhat subjective, it is not possible to say precisely how many phonemes there are in the English language, but there are around forty. The difficulty is that there are no hard dividing lines between similar sounds so that people's judgements will vary as to the point at which a word sounds like another one. Those judgements are likely to be coloured by the accent of the speaker and the background of the listener.

Because there are more phonemes than letters in the alphabet, phoneticians have devised special symbol sets to represent the phonemes. The commonest of these is the International Phonetic Alphabet (IPA). The objective is that there should be a unique symbol to represent each unique phoneme, and, being international, that implies every possible phoneme in all languages. The full table of IPA symbols therefore includes symbols to represent sounds which are never heard in English. Indeed some of the phonemes represented will not be heard in one English accent, but may be in another. Table 2.1 shows the common English phonetic symbols. The phonemes in the table are also grouped into different types, which will be explained later.

IPA symbol	Example	IPA symbol	Example		IPA symbol	Example	IPA symbol	Example
p	pet	tʃ	cheek		m	man	æ	at
b	bear	ʒ	rouge		n	nest	ɛː	care
t	ten	dʒ	jump		l	leaf	ɔː	horse
d	duck	ɹ	red		r	read	ɛ	end
k	kite	ŋ	sing		w	wind	ɪ	bit
g	goat	ɑ	arm		h	hand	ɔ	odd
s	sun	e	head		ʍ	whip	ʊ	foot
z	zebra	i	police		θ	thin	ə	ago
f	fish	o	old		ð	this	ʌ	up
v	voice	u	truth		ʃ	ship	ɜ	turn

Table 2.1   An extract of the IPA phonetic alphabet (the full alphabet includes sounds which do not occur in English).

Human Speech Production

Before we can look at how speech is synthesized, we must examine 'the real thing', which the synthesizer tries to imitate. There are two important kinds of sound in speech: *voiced* and *unvoiced*. Voicing is generated by the vocal cords. These are two flaps of tissue situated in the larynx in the throat. When exhaling, air passes between them, and they can be made to vibrate in that air stream, so producing a voiced sound. The pitch of the sound produced depends on tension in the vocal cords. Everyone's vocal cords have a characteristic **frequency** which is their most natural vibration frequency. This is normally lower in men than in women and children, but the speaker can control the tension in the vocal cords and hence alter the pitch of his or her speech. The pitch range of most adult males is around the range 50 to 250 Hz, while women's voices are usually around one octave higher, or 100 to 500 Hz (see Appendix C).

The speaker can control not only the pitch of voiced sounds but can also 'shape' the sounds generated by altering the shape of the cavities through which the sound travels on its way from the larynx to the mouth – by moving the tongue and reshaping the lips, for example (see Figure 2.1). Vowels are all voiced sounds produced with less constriction of the vocal tract, which vary in their production according to the shape of the mouth and lips. Just as the subjectivity of phonetics means that there is no agreement as to how many phonemes there are in the English language, different books identify different vowels, but the important point is that although there are only five vowel letters there are around fifteen vowel sounds, as shown in Table 2.1.

Glides are similar to vowels, in that they are voiced and continuous, but what distinguishes them is that they are *transitional*. The mouth shape (and hence the sound) is altered during their articulation.

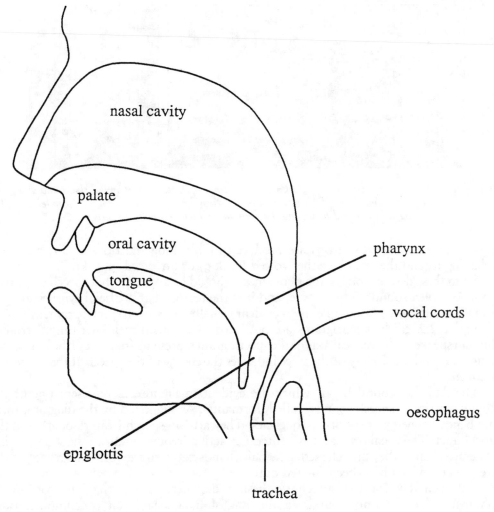

nasal cavity

palate

oral cavity

pharynx

tongue

vocal cords

oesophagus

epiglottis

trachea

Figure 2.1 The vocal tract.

The mouth is not the only cavity though which voiced sounds can pass; the nose too is important, and this gives rise to the *nasal* phonemes (m, n, and ŋ).

Unvoiced sounds are produced by air which is not vibrated by the vocal cords, but is made turbulent by being forced through a constriction. In the case of *aspirants* the constriction is formed by the vocal cords being held close together, but *not* set into vibration. In English h is the only aspirant. Other unvoiced sounds are generated by constrictions formed by the lips and teeth (f), the tongue tip and teeth (θ), the hard ridge just behind the front teeth (s) or the tongue further back along the palate (ʃ). These sounds are known as *fricatives*. Fricatives can be combined with voiced sounds, for example the phoneme z can be thought of as s with voicing.

So far all the sounds described have been produced by a continuous flow of air through the vocal tract. It is, however, possible to block the tract, so producing the

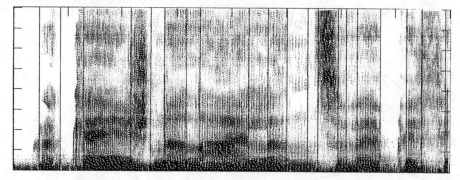

Figure 2.2   *A voice spectrogram. The darkness of the trace indicates the energy of the sound at a given frequency and time. Frequency increases vertically, while time progresses from left to right. The dark horizontal bands are the formants which characterize speech.*

sounds known as *stops*. Stops are produced by blocking the flow of air, and then releasing it, and they can be either voiced (b, d, g) or unvoiced (p, t, k).

From these descriptions of the phonemes it should be apparent that speech comprises some complex sounds. This is true, and it is the reason that artificial synthesis of the sounds is difficult. The complexity is evident visually in a speech spectrogram, as shown in Figure 2.2. Such spectrograms are produced by an instrument with input from a human speaker. The vertical axis of the spectrogram represents frequency, the horizontal axis time, and the density of the trace indicates the energy of the speech at that time and frequency.

The dark horizontal bands which are evident in Figure 2.2 represent one of the characteristics of speech sounds, called 'formants'. As suggested by the diagram, these are bands of energy at specific frequencies. They arise in speech from resonances in the vocal tract. The vocal tract acts as a filter, extracting frequencies from the sounds being generated before they are released. The paler bands between the formants represent the frequencies which have been filtered out.

Unfortunately for the speech synthesizer designer, to say that the forty-or-so phonemes are the only sounds in the English language is an oversimplification. Although those are the basic sounds, the way any individual speaks them varies depending on their context. As explained above, speech production involves the moving around of the speech organs (tongue, lips, etc.), and these are mechanical components of finite mass. Some sequences of movements of these organs are more difficult to perform, so that some sounds are easier to produce in sequence than others.

The effect of the influence of one phoneme on the pronunciation of the following one is called 'coarticulation'. There are quite subtle effects that occur in natural speech which often cannot be simulated in synthetic speech, leading to its sounding less realistic. The effect of coarticulation is probably most noticeable when comparing the pronunciation of a phoneme which occurs at the end of a word with the same one within a word. For example, the words 'construe' and 'constraint' begin with the same phonemes, but they may be pronounced differently because in the former case the speaker is likely to round his or her lips in anticipation of the ending u sound, while in saying constraint the lips will end quite open.

One approach to dealing with the problem of differing pronunciations of phonemes is to recognize that variations on the basic phonemes exist, which are known as *allophones*. They are *not* separate phonemes, because if one was substituted for the other in a word, that word would still be recognizable – it just might sound a little odd. As with phonemes, linguists disagree as to how many distinct allophones there are in the English language, but high-quality speech synthesizers have been developed on the basis of around sixty of them (May, 1982; Bruckert, 1984).

In addition to how the individual sounds or segments of speech are generated, speech also includes features which span segments: suprasegmental features. Writers often disagree about the terms to be used in discussing suprasegmental aspects of language. The way in which the terms are used in this book is therefore set out below. First, suprasegmental features are discussed as relating either to *prosody* or to *paralinguistics*.

Prosody and Paralinguistics

Prosody refers collectively to the qualities of stress, rhythm, timing and intonation. Stress refers to loudness (which is related to the **amplitude**) of the speech wave. It should not be confused with *accent*, which is used to describe a syllable which has been given prominence.[1] Stress is one of the characteristics which is increased to accent a syllable, but often other factors such as timing are much more important. In fact, analyses show that there is very little variation in the level of stress in normal speech. Shouted utterances are more stressed, but each word is still approximately equally stressed. Small differences in stress are used to great effect by combination with other variations. Rhythm arises from the pattern of syllables in the utterance. Rhythm is related to timing, where timing can refer to the duration of a syllable (or phoneme), but is also extremely important as applied to the duration of silence – pauses within the utterance. Intonation refers to the pitch patterns (or 'tune') of the speech.

It is very difficult to discuss the significance of prosodic features because as yet few theoretical foundations have been established. Rules must exist governing prosody, for if they did not how would speaker and listener agree on the significance of prosodic variations? For example, there is a rule in some dialects of English to the effect that rising pitch at the end of a sentence indicates that it is a question. That rule is understood by both the speaker and the listener, so that both recognize the significance of the intonation pattern and act accordingly (i.e. the listener will answer the question). However, the rules of prosody must be very complex, involving interactions between all of the above-mentioned qualities. The literature is full of examples with which writers succeed in supporting the proposition that the rules of prosody are complex, but which in so doing seem to make little progress toward disentangling those rules. It would be out of place here to digress into a detailed discussion of the difficulty of understanding prosody. Instead there is a brief discussion of some of the broad implications of prosody, followed by a small number of examples, to bring home the point that prosody is important.

---

[1] Notice that 'accent' is being used here *not* in the sense of regional variations in pronunciation. The distinction would be clear in a spoken context, according to which syllable of the word 'accent' was accented by the speaker!

One way of illustrating the difficulty of capturing prosody is to look at how we can try to impart prosodic information in written language – and how little we succeed. This will also be useful in the context of later sections in which we examine how to specify the text to be spoken by a speech synthesizer, the commonest method being to input the required text in a written form.

One of the purposes of punctuation of written text is to give an indication of the intended prosody, but this is by no means prescriptive. This is amply illustrated by the performance of plays. In interpreting the dialogue in a written script, an actor essentially fills in prosodic information which the playwright cannot communicate in the written script. The writer will have inserted as many cues as possible (or as felt necessary) in the form of punctuation, which may be supplemented by stage directions where punctuation is not sufficient. That still leaves enough room for interpretation, so that classic plays are produced repeatedly and audiences do not appear to become bored with them – partly because of the infinite possible variations in the verbal presentation.

The meaning of a sentence can be completely altered by variations in prosody. The simplest example is turning a statement:

It's raining.

into a question:

It's raining?

If spoken the difference in these two sentences would (in some dialects) be signalled by a falling intonation in the former example and a rising intonation in the second, and this is communicated to the reader by the use of the question mark.

The exclamation mark is more subtle and ambiguous.

It's raining!

clearly has a different significance from the earlier versions, but is the speaker expressing anger or excitement? If it was in a play and the difference significant, the writer might have to resort to stage directions:

[angrily] It's raining!

Commas may be used to indicate pauses; however, they give no means of suggesting the length of the pause. Some writers use the ellipsis ('. . .') to indicate a long pause. Again, the meaning of the same words can be changed radically, such as in

I think it's beautiful.

and

I think it's . . . beautiful.

Yet there is still ambiguity. Did the speaker pause because overawed by the beauty, or because his or her praise was reluctant?

The inclusion of direct speech is signalled textually by the use of quotation marks, and vocally through altering the timing and intonation. Thus the difference between

John said I went there on Sunday.

and

John said, 'I went there on Sunday.'

is most significant.

Accentuation of syllables is another important and subtle suprasegmental feature. In normal text the use of italics is really the only mechanism by which accent is communicated. If someone says, 'I thought Judith bought a *red* car', what they are paraphrasing is that they knew Judith had bought a car, but understood it to have been a red one. Whereas, if they were to say, 'I thought Judith bought a red *car*', they would be suggesting that they had misunderstood about what kind of vehicle she had bought. Emphasizing contrasts is just one of the uses of accent, and one of the simpler ones at that. The points to appreciate are that it is a means of the user communicating which parts of the utterance are particularly significant – and that it is very difficult to capture in written text.

As illustrated above, prosody is part of the information content of an utterance. Paralinguistic features, on the other hand, are less important in communicating information *from* the speaker, but relate more *about* the speaker. These features relate to the quality of the voice, which may for instance be creaky or breathy. This may communicate the emotional state of the speaker to the listener. (There is also a suggestion that breathiness may be an important feature which distinguishes female voices, see the section on quality, below.)

Why are suprasegmental features important? Is it vital to recreate the suprasegmental features of natural speech in synthetic speech? As shown above, the very meaning of an utterance can be completely altered by its suprasegmental structure but, furthermore, good suprasegmental structure improves the quality of the speech. Quality is itself an important feature, but one feature of good quality speech is that it is more pleasant to listen to. This requirement should not be underestimated for disabled users who may use a synthetic voice as their primary means of communication.

Body Language

Punctuation cannot capture all aspects of prosody. This limits the communication power of synthetic speech, but it should not be forgotten that normal conversation usually includes communication which is not expressed in the audible voice, but is non-vocal – often described as 'body language'. Although the voice is clearly the most important information-bearing component of speech, it is by no means the only one. Face-to-face communication relies also on other information which is communicated through posture, movement and eye contact. To take a crude example, a statement accompanied by a wink usually has its meaning reversed. More subtle messages are being passed all the time in unconscious body signals. In some cases the body language merely reinforces or confirms the auditory signal; in this case it may add emphasis but might be redundant. In other cases (such as the wink) the body language may alter the meaning of the spoken message.

A speech communicator alone cannot convey this extra information. Communicator users whose impairment is confined to their speech production mechanisms may be able to accompany their (synthetic) speech with appropriate gestures, in a quite natural manner. However, as has been stated previously, users of such devices commonly have more general physical impairments, which may prevent them from making the sort of subtle gestures associated with body language. Of course, communication through voice alone is by no means an unusual experience; anyone using a telephone has the same limitation. This probably explains why some people are quite uncomfortable about using telephones.

Formal sign languages can be considered to be an aspect of body language, which should not be forgotten. Many people who have speech impairments are taught sign languages (such as Makaton); they are by no means confined to use by deaf people. A communicator user who has been taught sign language is quite likely to accompany the speech with signs which will help to clarify his or her message, at least to a listener who also uses signs.

Much of the discussion above relates to the problem of ambiguity. For instance, we have seen how a given written sentence can be read in different ways (applying different prosody) so changing its meaning. Ambiguity in this context may be seen therefore as undesirable, but let us not over-generalize this sentiment: without ambiguity there would be no art. A poem would soon become boring if it could be written down in such a way that there would be only one possible way of reading it.

This section has given a very brief introduction to human speech production. It has explained some of the main features of speech in terms of the physical apparatus which produces it. A speech synthesizer is composed of very different components but should be capable of simulating the same effects. The next section outlines how current synthesizers attempt to do this.

Speech Synthesis

To synthesize speech it is necessary to have the facility to generate sounds similar to those in human speech and to control their production. The approaches to these problems are explained below, but first it is worth pointing out that there are two approaches to controlling synthetic speech production, which can be described as *copy synthesis* and *synthesis-by-rule*. Copy synthesis amounts to making a recording of a human speaker, storing it in an encoded form and then using that stored code to drive a sound generator. Synthesis-by-rule, on the other hand, is more of a pure form of synthesis, since no human speaker need ever have been involved. The speech is produced from some abstract representation – such as written text.

Sound can be represented as a waveform. A waveform can be represented graphically, as in Figure 2.3. The curve in that diagram can be said to be an **analogue** representation of the wave because it varies in a continuous fashion, whereby the distance of the curve from the horizontal axis is always proportional to the amplitude of the sound it represents. Sounds are often represented and stored in an analogue form: the shape of the groove in a gramophone record is an analogue of the sounds recorded, for instance.

There are computers which operate in an analogue manner, but they are today quite rare. The important development has been in **digital** technology. The description of 'digital' arises from the fact that computers deal with numbers. This point is often made in explaining how computers work. Yet to some people it obscures the power of computers because it implies that computers are useful only in mathematical

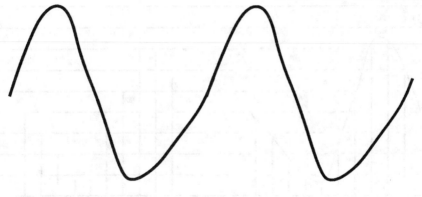

Figure 2.3   A sound wave.

applications. In fact, because in principle all forms of information can be converted into a numerical form they can be processed by computers. In other words it is the *interpretation* placed on the numbers in the computer which is important. For example, written text can be easily converted to numbers and hence processed by a computer. As far as the computer on which this book has been word processed is concerned, the word 'sample' is the set of numbers, 115 97 109 112 108 101, but the **software** is written in such a way that it will display that data as the letters s a m p l e on the computer screen or on paper via a printer. In other words the software effectively imposes an interpretation on the numbers.

A vast technology has evolved to process digital information, the most general-purpose piece of digital technology being the computer. Very powerful facilities are available to process any information which is in a digital form. Hence, if speech (or other sound) is converted into a digital form, it too can be processed using this technology. The availability of such powerful technology opens up great new possibilities regarding the processing and reproduction of sound.

To create an analogue representation of a waveform its amplitude must be measured constantly in time. In principle an analogue representation is exact. That is to say that between any two points on the curve in Figure 2.3 there is an infinite number of distinct intermediate points, so that it should be possible to say exactly what the amplitude of the wave is at any precise point in time (though in practice the accuracy of measuring devices is limited so that no analogue will be exact, and the number of points representable is finite).

The first step to representing a waveform digitally involves *not* measuring it constantly, but *sampling* it at intervals. In other words, the amplitude is measured, then a fixed time period elapses and then the amplitude is again measured. After the same length of pause a third sample is obtained, and so on. Such sampling of one cycle of the wave in Figure 2.3 is illustrated in Figure 2.4. Digital representation makes an explicit assumption that the waveform cannot be stored exactly, so that each of the samples A to J in Figure 2.4 would be stored as the number *nearest* to its amplitude. This is called 'quantization'. Reading the numbers off for each of the samples in Figure 2.4, we obtain the digital representation of the original waveform, as given in Table 2.2.

Transforming a waveform into a digitized representation does involve the possibility

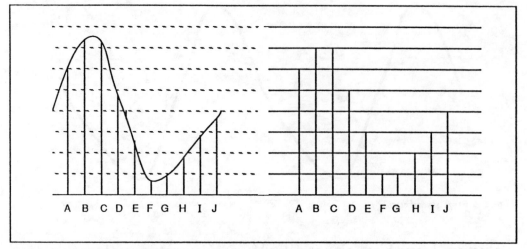

Figure 2.4   *Sampling. The height of the wave is measured off at regular intervals. Notice that the samples are measured on a fixed scale, as shown by the dotted horizontal lines.*

of distorting it, such that it does not accurately reflect the shape of the original waveform. For example, if one traced the outline of the tops of the vertical lines in the quantized waveform on the right of Figure 2.4 the shape would not be exactly that on the left, because the lines are set to lengths equal to the nearest whole number. One way of improving the fidelity of the quantized wave is to increase the accuracy of the quantization. In other words, if the example waveform had been quantized to the nearest tenth of a unit, then the lengths would not have to be rounded up or down to the nearest whole number, which would mean samples B and C would be more closely represented. Storing more precise numbers requires a greater amount of storage; just as the number 1 can be represented using fewer digits than the number 1.1.

A	6
B	7
C	7
D	5
E	3
F	1
G	1
H	2
I	3
J	4

Table 2.2   *The numbers which would represent the digitized form of the wave illustrated in Figure 2.4*

Another potential distortion arises from the fact that the quantized representation contains no information as to the shape of the waveform between samples. This effect can be reduced by decreasing the delay between samples, which is equivalent to increasing the sampling frequency. In fact, it is relatively easy to prove that no information is actually lost as long as the waveform is sampled at a frequency which is at least *twice* that of the waveform's highest frequency.[1] Again, improving the quality of the digitized waveform implies a cost in terms of extra memory – and hence increased cost – since more numbers need to be stored.

Having transformed the sound into that digital representation it can be stored and processed by using normal digital technology. Now spoken words can be stored in computer memory and rapidly recalled at random, just as the written words of a text can be rapidly accessed by a **word processor**. The best musical recordings are made nowadays using digital techniques.

Problems which analogue techniques have, which are (to a large extent) avoided by digital techniques, are distortion and **noise**. Every time an analogue waveform is processed its shape changes slightly because of imperfections in the equipment. The analogue representation (be it a groove on a record, an electrical signal or whatever) cannot be *exactly* the same shape as the original waveform. Also, as the waveform is processed by different pieces of equipment (the microphone, the tape recorder, the speaker, etc.), that equipment will introduce traces of signal which were not part of the original wave. These effects are inevitable with even the best quality analogue equipment. However, once a sound has been digitized, such changes do not occur; if the numbers representing the digitized waveform in Figure 2.4 (i.e. the numbers in Table 2.2) are copied from one device to another they will be copied *exactly*. Apparent distortions might be introduced through imperfections in transmission of the information, but because of quantization these will be ironed out. For example, if a device receives the number 5.9, that is not a valid level and it can be assumed that it should be 6 and will be corrected accordingly.

This form of direct digitization of sounds is referred to as 'pulse code modulation', or PCM. Using PCM to digitize speech sounds using a sufficiently high sampling rate does imply storing a lot of numbers. For example, telephone systems are designed to handle sounds with frequencies up to 3,400 Hz. That implies that to digitize telephone-quality speech, the sampling frequency must be at least 6,800 Hz, or more realistically 10,000 Hz to avoid aliasing. Supposing an eight-**bit** number is used to represent each sample (giving 256 possible quantum levels), it would take 80,000 bits or 10,000 **bytes** of computer memory to store one second of speech. That is the same amount of memory as would be needed to store about five pages of a paperback book.

As mentioned above, memory is always a limiting factor of computers because memory costs money. So, it is desirable to reduce the memory requirements as far as possible. It is in fact possible to reduce the number of samples stored without losing appreciable quality by applying mathematical, *data-compression* techniques to the

---

[1] In practice, sampling frequencies slightly above the minimum are used, so as to avoid an effect known as 'aliasing', which can introduce phantom frequencies into the reproduced sound which were not in the original.

samples. Given the power of digital technology, it is a relatively simple matter to apply such techniques to a sampled waveform.

One simple form of data compression is *delta modulation*. This technique exploits the fact that it is more efficient to store the *difference* between successive samples than their absolute values. The data are then decoded by adding each difference to a 'running total'. Since the numbers involved will be smaller they can be represented by fewer digits, and so save on memory space. Further economies can be attained by using a technique whereby only changes in the slope of the input waveform are recorded (known as 'adaptive pulse coded modulation', or APCM): a more positive (steeper upward) slope is encoded as a 1, and a more negative slope as a 0. By applying this kind of technique the data rate to store reasonable quality speech can be reduced to 16,000 bits per second or, for good quality speech, 32,000 bits per second, somewhat less than half the overhead for PCM.

Still better compression factors can be attained by using the technique of linear predictive coding (LPC). This technique exploits the fact that speech waveforms contain a high degree of redundancy and are very predictable. Without going into mathematical details, it is based on the fact that it is possible to show that the value of (say) the hundredth sample (s_{100}) can be predicted from the previous fifty samples (s_{50} ... s_{99}), so that it is not necessary to store the hundredth sample (s_{100}). In other words, the information contained in s_{100} is redundant. Using techniques based on this approach it is possible to reduce the data rate to as low as 10,000 bits per second.

Digitized speech is generally used as the basis of copy-synthesis systems. Essentially, what is done is that a recording of a human speaker is made which can be played back at any time, under the control of the computer. In fact the 'recording' consists of a set of numbers describing the speech which is used to drive the synthesizer output. In general, the elements recorded may be whole sentences or phrases, or words. If individual words are stored, the computer can string them together to make new sentences. Most people have probably heard both types of speech when they have dialled a disconnected phone number. A message is played saying something like: 'The number you have dialled is no longer in use. The number you should dial is 667676.' The first part of the message sounds natural and flowing, but then the digits of the number are spoken as clipped, unnatural sounds. Of course, what is happening is that the machine is stringing together digitized recordings of the numbers.

As already explained, reproduction of digitized speech is generally of high quality. The major disadvantage is that it is limited in its vocabulary. For instance, if the speech is stored as words then only those words can be spoken; words not among those stored simply cannot be pronounced. There are applications in which such a prescribed vocabulary is quite adequate, examples being talking watches and calculators. Some systems allow developers to make their own digitized recordings and store the appropriate data, while some manufacturers will undertake to do that for customers. Even so, once the vocabulary has been established and placed in memory that defines the limits of the device's language.

It is not necessary to store whole words, however. Recordings can be made of phonemes, and these strung together to create words. Such devices have an unlimited vocabulary, but will have a lower quality of speech. (Digitized speech has also been used as the basis of diphone synthesis, which is described in the next section.)

Human voice production, as described earlier, can be viewed as the production of a

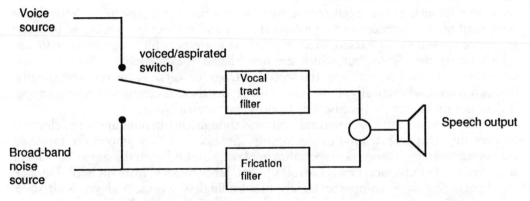

Figure 2.5   A resonance synthesizer. Two sources of sound are used, one corresponding to voiced phonemes and the other which produces aspirated 'hissing' sounds.

signal (voice sounds) which is filtered by the cavities of the vocal tract. Another approach to synthesis of speech is based upon building electrical circuits which simulate this signal-filtering process. An electrical signal consisting of a broad range of frequencies is generated, corresponding to the voiced sound. This is filtered through a circuit to produce a signal with the banded formant structure, and that is then converted into an acoustic signal (i.e. audible speech) in an electrical speaker.

The system described above deals only with voiced sounds; what about unvoiced ones? Recall that aspirants also originate at the vocal cords, though the cords are *not* set into vibration. The aspirated sound passes through the same vocal tract filters as a voiced sound, and the same kind of formant structure is produced. Within a filter-based synthesizer, therefore, aspirants can be generated by replacing the voiced signal input to the filters by a **broad-band noise** source which effectively generates a hissing signal, as shown in the upper part of Figure 2.5.

Fricatives are different in that they are not generated at the vocal cords, but in the mouth. These can be approximated by high-frequency noise, the central frequency of which can be controlled by a variable filter, to generate sounds corresponding to each of the fricatives. Recall that fricatives may be voiced, so Figure 2.5 shows that voiced and fricative sounds can be generated simultaneously and summed together.

This section has presented a summary of some of the common techniques used to generate sounds which approximate those found in speech. There is a certain amount of confidentiality surrounding some of the commercially available synthesizers, and it may be that some variations on these techniques are employed. In the next section we look at how those sound generators are controlled, how the user can specify what is to be spoken.

Generating Speech from Text

Analysis of language is often divided into the study of syntax and semantics. Syntax refers to the *grammar* of the language, the rules governing what is correct, while semantics refers to the *meaning* of utterances in the language. Written English syntax includes rules such as that a sentence must contain a finite verb, the initial letter of the first word of the sentence must be a capital letter and it must be terminated by a full stop, question mark or exclamation mark. It is quite possible to generate sentences which satisfy these rules but which are nevertheless meaningless – which is where semantics steps in. For example, the sentence 'Dogs are cats.' is correct syntactically. Though correct syntactically, however, to the reader there is clearly something wrong: it does not make sense – because it is incorrect semantically.

As with so many aspects of natural language, though, distinctions are not as clear cut as they might appear from this description. Syntax is a very important factor in conveying meaning, while poets specialize in playing around with the supposed rules of the language. For instance, Lewis Carroll's poem 'Jabberwocky' from his book *Through the Looking-Glass* is composed largely of meaningless words, and yet with some recognizable words to provide syntactic clues readers have the impression that they understand the poem.

> *'Twas brillig, and the slithy toves*
> *Did gyre and gimble in the wabe;*
> *All mimsy were the borogoves,*
> *And the mome raths outgrabe.*

Syntax includes the rules of punctuation, and these serve to assist the reader to understand the meaning of the language, as mentioned earlier in the discussion of suprasegmental features of speech.

In general, computers are better able to analyse the syntactic structure of written language than its semantics. To a large extent the syntax can be expressed as a set of well-defined rules, and computers operate on the basis of sets of rules. However, when it comes to semantics the rules are much more complex and it is a question of philosophical debate whether a computer could ever be said to *understand* the meaning of language (which might be easier to discuss if the philosophers could agree as to what understanding is in people!).

The earlier example ('Dogs are cats') illustrates this well. For a computer to verify the syntax of the sentence it would first have to perform a lexical analysis, categorizing the component words as 'subject', 'verb' and 'object' and then it would check rules such as:

1. Does it start with a capital letter?
2. Is it terminated by a full stop?
3. Is there a finite verb?
4. Does the verb have a subject and object?
5. Do the number and person of the subject agree with the verb?

More important in analysing text to be translated into speech (and more difficult to achieve), is to be able to identify the syntactic components of an utterance: What are the subject, the verb and the object? If there is an adjective in the utterance does it apply to the subject or the object? – and suchlike. It is this level of analysis which can be used to give 'hints' to the computer as to the meaning of the utterance. However, such hints are not enough; it is also necessary to analyse the semantics. To specify that an utterance is incorrect semantically implies a certain degree of knowledge, not only of the language, but of the world. In other words, it is necessary to understand that dogs and cats are different species of animals, and to recognize the difference between that sentence and the following: 'Lions are cats.'

In generating speech from written text the computer can make use of the syntactic cues of punctuation, but some anomalies cannot be resolved without the assistance of semantics. Most of the discussion below is therefore based on syntactic analysis of input text and we will see some of the problems caused by lack of accessible semantic cues.

Natural speech is the goal to which all speech synthesis systems aspire. However, it is important to make clear that the current stage of development is far from achieving that aim. In the discussions below three factors will become clear: suprasegmental features of speech are very difficult to synthesize; the most useful form of input to a synthesizer is normal text; and all input technologies are very slow. These factors all lead to the conclusion that *synthetic speech is audible writing*.

What are the building blocks (phonemes, words, sentences, etc.) out of which synthetic speech should be generated? In general, the larger the units, the more naturalness can be attained but the less the degree of flexibility. For instance, if whole sentences are stored (as LPC parameters, for instance) then the pronunciation of the component words will be correct including coarticulation effects and the prosody of the sentence will be captured too, but the synthesizer would be confined to very specific utterances. For instance, the sentence 'I would like a cup of coffee' could be stored and reproduced exactly, but the user would be frustrated if he or she actually preferred tea. Greater flexibility would be achieved by building utterances from pre-stored words. A large number of sentences could be constructed. Assuming each of the words of the sentence above was stored individually plus the word 'tea', the user could now be more choosy. However, there would generally be a loss of quality, because the words would have to be strung together and this would not take account of the coarticulation effects or prosody of natural speech. The vocabulary of such a system would still be limited; it could not generate a word which it had not been specifically programmed to say – 'tea' and 'coffee' might be available but not 'beer', for example.

Total flexibility is achieved if phonemes are used as the building blocks. In principle, a synthesizer which has been programmed with the appropriate data to produce the forty-odd phonemes of the English language can generate any word in the language. The problem is again how to string the components (the phonemes) together, making the transitions between them sound natural. Coarticulation effects are even more significant at this level of construction of speech. Techniques have been devised to smooth the transition between synthesized phonemes, which simulate some coarticulation effects.

One coarticulation effect which has been mentioned is the production of allophones. This can be simulated by making the allophone the unit of synthesis. In other words, the number of sounds which can be generated is expanded from forty phonemes to around sixty allophones and the synthesis rules are made more complex to select the appropriate allophone, depending on its context.

Another approach is based on the observation that the transitions between phonemes are critical in speech, as has already been discussed in the context of coarticulation. Therefore, instead of storing individual phonemes, pairs of phonemes should be analysed. Such units are called 'diphones'. They can be constructed by recording natural speech, extracting transitions between phonemes and encoding them as LPC coefficients which can then be treated mathematically.

One apparent problem of diphone-based synthesis is the number of diphones which must be stored. If there are forty phonemes there are potentially $40^2 = 1,600$ diphones. Fortunately, though, many phoneme pairs do not occur in natural language – because they are difficult to pronounce together. This means that good-quality speech can be generated based on around 1,000 diphones (see Boubekker, Foulds and Norman, 1986). Diphone-based synthesis is discussed further below, in the next section: Quality.

Generating speech in a copy synthesis system amounts to specifying which of its stored elements is to be retrieved and generated. For example an LPC-based system may (re-)produce words from a stored vocabulary. The user may specify the next word as a code (i.e. effectively specifying 'Speak word number 60'), though that code may be generated automatically – when the user touches a particular square on a word board or key on a calculator, for instance.

A more difficult problem is to generate words from a phoneme-based synthesizer. The user could specify the phonemes to be generated much as in the example above (e.g. 'Speak phonemes 42, 37, 101'), but it is easier if the facility exists to enter the phonemes in a textual form. One possible form of input is the sort of notation presented in Table 2.1, where the phonemes are represented by visual graphemes (letters). Relatively simple software can be developed which will perform such a grapheme-to-code translation. One advantage of this approach is that the user can experiment with different phoneme strings to produce the best pronunciation. However, the obvious disadvantage is that the user must be trained in phonetics in order to generate the input stream of symbols.

Of much more general use is a system in which the user can specify the text to be spoken in a normal written form. One approach would be for the system to contain tables of all the words to be generated, and their corresponding phonetic translations. This has obvious disadvantages: it would restrict the vocabulary and it would involve a large amount of memory to store the table.

Better, then, is an approach whereby the phonetic translation can be deduced automatically from the written text. However, programs which can do this are not trivial. The extent of the problem can be envisaged if it is compared with the task of teaching a child to read – except that computers are not as intelligent as children. The child is first taught phonetic values of the letters of the alphabet (æ, b, k, etc.). The child is then in a position to construct (some) words from their written form. So for instance, on seeing the word 'cat' the child constructs the phonemes k, æ, t. He or she also learns that some letter combinations have particular phonetic values, for example that *ph* is pronounced f and *sh* is ʃ. Unfortunately, reading is not that simple, particularly in a language like English which is not phonetic. For no apparent reason the rules the child has just learned are often broken. If the child has learned that *c* is pronounced k, then how will he or she pronounce 'city'? Another rule is then taught, along the lines that if a word starts with *ci* the *c* is pronounced s. The more rules the child can master, the better his or her reading – and yet that is still not enough. Some English pronunciations follow no rules at all. The best example is the suffix -ough. What rule could explain the differences in the pronunciation of the following words: though, enough, bough and borough? Some words remain irregular exceptions, the pronunciation of which can be taught only individually.

The best text-to-speech systems employ a combination of the techniques above. They include a dictionary of *exceptions* – words whose pronunciation is so irregular that their correct pronunciation cannot be deduced from their spelling. Though, enough, bough and borough will be in there, along with words like 'women' and 'of' (the only word in English in which *f* is pronounced **v**) which we read every day without thinking about how odd their pronunciation is. The exception dictionary can also be used to ensure that common abbreviations are spoken intelligibly. For example, 'Mr' and 'Mrs' would be expanded and spoken as normal words (i.e. mɪstəɹ and mɪsɪz). Some very common words may also be included in the dictionary, even though their pronunciation may be quite regular, simply as a means of speeding up the translation.

If a word is not in the exception dictionary, it is assumed to follow the rules of normal pronunciation, and a phoneme string will be generated for it. Of course that assumption may not be valid, the word may just have been omitted from the dictionary, which can lead to pronunciations which are amusing – or baffling. The bigger the exception dictionary the less likely this is to occur and so the better the pronunciation in general. One of the best synthesizers currently available, the Dectalk, has a built-in dictionary of 6,000 entries (Bruckert, 1984). That is supplemented by a user-definable dictionary of up to 150 entries, allowing users to ensure that irregular words which they use frequently but which are not in the built-in dictionary will be pronounced correctly. Having a larger dictionary also entails disadvantages, of course: first, the requirement for more memory to contain the dictionary costs money; second, it will take longer to search a large dictionary. Speed of search can be very important as it can affect the speech. It is therefore important that efficient search methods are employed.

Ideally, looking up words in the dictionary should not be carried out on a simple word-by-word match. Words which are not in the dictionary, but which can be derived from those which are, ought not to be missed. For example, assuming the word 'borough' is in the dictionary, the look-up program should not reject 'boroughs' just

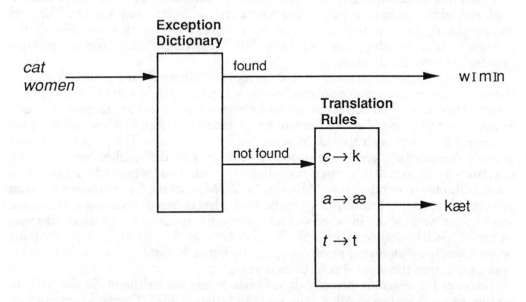

Figure 2.6   *A schematic diagram of the translation of text into speech. Spellings are first looked up in the exception dictionary. If the word is in the dictionary its pronunciation is extracted directly (as for 'women'). Words not in the dictionary are assumed to be regular in their pronunciation, which can then be derived from the translation rules (as for 'cat').*

because it has an extra 's' appended. Dictionaries are therefore often based on *morphemes*, where a morpheme is the smallest unit of language having a meaning. Under such a scheme 'borough' might be treated as the morphemes {borough} and {-s}.

So, the pronunciation of any words which are truly not represented in the dictionary ought to be derivable from their spelling, according to the built-in rules. Again, the more rules there are the better the pronunciation will be. Figure 2.6 is a block diagram of the main stages of text-to-speech translation.

Sometimes, despite the best efforts of the text-to-speech translator, a word will still be generated with a gross mispronunciation. In some applications human intervention may be called upon at this point. The user may re-enter the word, deliberately misspelling it to give it the appropriate phonetic value.

Actually one further level of processing is likely to be applied to the input text *before* any of the translations described above. Initially it is likely to be reformatted into a more 'readable' form. For instance, it is generally better to have £42 spoken as 'forty-two pounds' rather than 'pound four two'. Problems occur in this stage of translation too, though. For example, standard computer characters are sometimes used in more than one way. Is a '-' being used as a dash or a minus sign? It should be possible to deduce this from the context, but it does imply further work. Similarly, the same character is used as the single quotation mark and the apostrophe.

Unfortunately, even with all this processing, some words will not be pronounced correctly. For example, the verb 'read' can be pronounced as either 'red' or 'reed' (**red** or **rid**), depending on its tense. A program which could distinguish these cases would have to have some level of understanding of the text. In other words, it would have to perform a semantic analysis. This is beyond the capabilities of most current systems.

Generating speech sounds from written has been likened above to teaching a child to read, and adding prosody is part of the actor's craft in interpreting a script. The rules for translating written text to speech are complex, but we have suggested that researchers have perhaps been less successful in deriving similar rules to generate appropriate prosodic structure.

It has been suggested by some researchers (notably Chomsky and Halle, 1968) that the accent component of prosody can be induced from a purely syntactical analysis of speech. They have derived a set of rules which they claim capture assignment of accent. However, others have displayed examples of utterances which would sound quite unnatural if spoken with the accent suggested by those rules. This is partly because prosody depends to a great extent on the intentions of the speaker, which cannot effectively be captured in written text. Indeed, it has been suggested that accent is predictable only to mind-readers (Bolinger, 1972)! Most of the research which has been carried out on adding prosody to synthetic speech has therefore been based on manual specification of prosody. In other words, a person has specified the prosodic structure by use of special notations within the input. This is analogous to the user specifying pronunciation by inputting phoneme symbols, but it is similarly desirable in many applications that the input should be as normal text.

The rules for assigning prosody, based on a purely textual input, in the MITalk synthesizer are described in Allen, Hunnicutt and Klatt (1987). These rules govern four aspects of prosody: stress, duration, pitch and allocation of allophones. Although accented syllables are perceived as stressed – of greater intensity – the measured increased intensity is very small. Stress decreases at the end of an utterance, especially if the syllable is unaccented. There is a model for predicting segment durations. First of all, it is assumed that the prosodic boundaries – at which segments are longer in duration – can be determined from the syntactic structure of a sentence. Accent is assigned to syllables according to a set of rules, or from entries in a lexicon. The model of segment duration is then based upon the following assumptions:

1. Each phonetic segment type has an inherent duration, which is one of its distinctive properties.
2. There is a set of rules (see below) which effect a percentage increase or decrease in the duration of the segment.
3. Segments cannot be compressed beyond a certain minimum duration.

The model can be summarized by the following formula:

$$\text{Duration} = D_{min} + \frac{(D_{inherent} - D_{min}) \times S}{100}$$

Where: $D_{inherent}$ is the inherent duration of the segment
D_{min} is the minimum duration of a segment, if accented
S is the percentage shortening.

The value of the shortening, S, is determined from a set of rules. There are eleven of them, including the following examples:

1. The vowel in the syllable just before a pause is lengthened.
2. Consonants in non-word-initial position are shortened.
3. Segments are shortened in consonant–consonant sequences.

Many researchers describe pitch in terms of a contour, which is almost like the *tune* of an utterance. MITalk deduces the form of the pitch contour by analysis of the accent allocation of syllables, although it is conceded that trying to apply rules to such an analysis can be frustrating 'because one depends on sentence analysis routines to determine aspects of syntactic structure or semantic importance, and these routines are often wrong' (Allen, Hunnicutt and Klatt, 1987, p. 763).

Not only is prosody important in terms of communication, but it also has an important subjective effect on the perceived acceptability of synthesized speech. It has been suggested that to reduce the fatigue of long-term exposure to speech *any* variation in stress and intonation can be better than none – even if it is not correctly located (Elovitz, Johnson, McHugh and Shore, 1976). This implies that even randomly assigned prosody is less wearing than none!

There are applications for which it is arguable whether sophisticated automatic prosody is a desirable feature. Just as an actor can shade the meaning of a script through changes in the prosody of its presentation, so a program might appear to interpret a text. This might, for instance, prejudice someone reading a book through a reading machine, in a way that a person reading the text visually would not be influenced.

Recall the earlier statement that in most applications it is desirable that the input should be in the form of normal printable text. In the case of receptive communication, such as a reading machine for blind users, it is clear that the input will be text as printed in books, so that the restriction on input will be strict. There may be some flexibility for expressive communication, though. Plainly, text input has the advantage that it requires minimal training (at least for users who are already literate). However, just as the user may sometimes resort to helping the system with its pronunciation by re-spelling a difficult word, he or she might also give it extra hints to help it to assign prosodic structure. The input will no longer be in the form of plain text, but may be supplemented by commands or marks which specify prosodic variations in the manner the utterance should be spoken. These commands will be *embedded* in the stream of phonemes. In other words, the sound generator hardware accepts a stream of input; if it encounters a phoneme in the stream it generates the corresponding sound, but it will also encounter commands for which it does not generate any sound, but it changes the value of one of its internal states.

Quality

The term 'quality' applied to synthetic speech refers to its closeness to natural speech. The discussion above of human speech production should give some impression of why it is so difficult to create human-sounding speech. The ultimate test of a speech synthesizer might be if it were indistinguishable from a human speaker. As it is, researchers have been content with devising less demanding evaluation schemes. In general these amount to subjective assessment of intelligibility. They may include tests of identification of isolated phonemes as well as complete utterances of words or sentences.

There is no accepted standard test of speech synthesizers. The American organization, the Institution of Electrical and Electronics Engineers (IEEE) did publish a recom-mended practice for speech quality measurements in 1969 (IEEE, 1969), but this has never been widely adopted as the basis of standardized testing. This lack of an agreed testing procedure is unfortunate as it means that potential buyers cannot apply objective comparisons, and are somewhat reliant on manufacturers' documentation and advertising.

No existing rule-based synthesizer would come close to passing the test of being indistinguishable from natural speech. Obviously intelligibility is one factor in passing such a test, and many aspects of synthetic speech relating to intelligibility have already been mentioned above. However, the term quality is used here to refer also to those aspects of speech production which go beyond mere intelligibility. These are harder to define – and harder to achieve – in some cases because we do not yet fully appreciate their significance. As has been stated before, speech is a very rich medium involving a high degree of redundancy, and though speech can be synthesized which omits some of the redundant features but is nevertheless understandable, the loss of quality may be significant.

Many people hearing synthetic speech for the first time are surprised by its low quality. They usually find it very hard to understand and imagine that it could never be a viable means of communication. However, the importance of quality depends very much on the use to which the speech is being applied – and on the relative importance of balancing factors, such as cost. Good quality is most critical where synthetic speech is being used for expressive communication by a non-vocal person. In other applications there is usually more leeway with regard to quality.

A person's voice is an important part of his or her personality. Think of the importance of the voice of a character in a radio play. Another illustration is the reaction of some people on hearing their own voice as replayed on a tape recorder: they can be shocked and upset that their voice does not sound as they would like it to; it does not conform to their self-image. Even the best current synthesizers are of such low quality that they inevitably detract from a person's persona. It is not surprising that some individuals choose to use other means of communication, because of the low quality of the available speech. Though it must be acknowledged that the features which make up quality can be so subtle that they are very difficult to capture, it is unfortunate that developers do not seem to realize how important they are to this particular group of users.

Quality is often less important to receptive speech users. Listeners usually learn quite quickly to accommodate to the idiosyncrasies of speech synthesizers, so that quality and, particularly, intelligibility become less important. Other properties of the synthesizer may be rather more important, such as price and speed. An example would be the blind user who said that he would rather have low quality at half price, than high quality at twice the price.

Cost is an interesting aspect of a speech synthesizer. Better-quality synthesizers will include more complex and expensive hardware but, as should be clear from the previous discussion, the main component affecting quality is the software. Software is notoriously difficult to price. There is no raw material to be paid for, just the labour of teams of programmers. Yet programs usually grow and develop over a long period, and it is hard to estimate the effort that has gone into them. For example, the software which performs the text-to-speech translation in one of the leading commercial synthesizers has an ancestry which can be traced back over twenty years. Once a program has been completed it can be copied indefinitely at essentially no additional cost. At the same time, much of the software development has been carried out as part of academic research and it would be unrealistic to expect to recoup all the development costs. Hence, pricing is a matter of marketing policy. People will pay more for better quality. However manufacturers can undercut their rivals by narrowing their profit margins in the hope of selling greater volumes.

Another relevant difference between expressive and receptive users is the person who listens to the speech. For an expressive user, the listener can be anybody – including people who have had no previous exposure to synthetic speech. Receptive users, on the other hand, listen to the voice themselves. They have the opportunity – and probably the motivation – to learn to understand and tolerate the voice. Improvements in perceived intelligibility are observed to occur quite rapidly with training.

Many quite gross qualitative features of speech have still not been successfully addressed. For example, the vast majority of speech synthesizers have male voices. (The Dectalk is one exception, having female voices in its selection.) This alone may deter many would-be female users, particularly if they need a voice prosthesis. The difference between male and female voices is more complex than just their frequency range. A good-quality female voice cannot be generated by simply modifying the parameters applied to a male-voice synthesizer. Whether a female voice is inherently more difficult to synthesize, or whether the same amount of effort has not been applied to the development of a female-voice synthesizer by engineers who are predominantly male, is a moot point.

Such bias is also apparent in the area of accent and dialect. Most English-language synthesizers have American accents, having been developed in the United States. One well-known British user of a speech communicator has a frequently used sentence quickly accessible in his word selection system, which is 'Please excuse my American accent.' This is not to be xenophobic about American accents, they are just inappropriate for non-American expressive users. Indeed there are probably many American users of speech systems who might prefer to have an accent corresponding to their home region of the country. Similarly, synthesizer development for many languages other than English is not as well advanced.

One important aspect of quality might best be described as *pleasantness*. Essentially, this is meant to describe that quality which makes a voice suitable for listening to over long periods. This may be most important for anyone who is expected to make any kind of extensive use of synthetic speech – either expressively or receptively. This is, of course, a subtle and subjective characteristic. Hopefully, it is one which will improve with development of better synthesizers and better understanding of speech. Even so, it is likely that it will always be desirable that users can control speech output, to select different voices and to adjust the speech to suit their own tastes.

Speed can be a very important characteristic of speech. Most conversations proceed at about 150 words per minute. That is a comfortable rate for most people to produce speech. However, it is quite possible to understand speech at much higher rates. Artificially accelerated speech loses quality. Once again, therefore, the importance of the ability to adjust the speed of speech production depends on the use to which it is being put. An expressive user is likely to want speech at a natural rate, which also implies that it will be at its best quality. However, a receptive user may be more interested in maximizing the flow of information and so will want a faster rate – accepting the consequent degradation in quality.

In most applications for people other than receptive users increased speed is not a necessary facility. Designers generally aim to achieve conversational speeds. As should be clear from the earlier discussions, the limiting factor on attainable speed is the amount of processing carried out – which also influences the quality of the speech. There is a need for designers to be made more aware that speed is a very important characteristic for some users, and effort ought to be expended on achieving high-quality speech at a faster rate.

Speed of speech reproduction is less of a problem for expressive users. Since their main requirement is to take part in conversation, natural speech rates are appropriate. Also, as is discussed more fully in the next chapter, the limiting factor on speed is the rate at which they can specify the input.

Another technique for increasing the speed is to reduce the number of words in each utterance. This can be done in the same way as composers of telegrams tend to do, removing less important words, such as the articles. Once more this is possible because of the redundancy in the language. The Dolphin Apollo synthesizer has this feature built in.

What can be done to improve quality? The continuing improvement in the quality of computer hardware, accompanied by lowering of costs, can only assist the improvement of speech quality. More complex rules and larger exception dictionaries can become viable if larger memory and faster **processors** are available. At the same time, further progress in many of the fields of research discussed above will lead to better quality. For instance, lack of quality is often manifested in the suprasegmental features of speech. As these become better understood, more comprehensive rules will be devised and better prosody achieved.

Another area of research that promises to lead to improvements in voice quality and articulation is based on an approach to synthesis which is completely different from those described earlier. The idea is that the synthesizer should be based on a mathematical model of the vocal tract. A mathematical model is built by deriving sets of equations which reflect the behaviour of the system it represents. The model is normally implemented as a computer program since the computer can quickly perform the calculations to solve the equations. The user can then perform experiments on the model and hence predict how the real system would behave in particular circumstances.

An example of mathematical modelling is that modern weather forecasting depends upon computer-based models of the atmosphere. The 'experiments' that meteorologists do essentially comprise their feeding the data describing the weather on one day into their computer model and asking, 'Given these circumstances what will the weather be like the following day?' They can then feed in the data for today, and find out what will happen tomorrow. Of course cynics might suggest that this example is a bad one because forecasts are so often wrong. If that is the case, it merely highlights one of the problems of modelling – that of building a sufficiently accurate model.

The idea of vocal tract modelling is to build a mathematical representation of the vocal tract, as illustrated in Figure 2.1, with components corresponding to each of the features shown there: larynx, tongue, lips, etc. Then, by effectively placing all of the components of the model in a given configuration it should be possible to generate the sound which the human vocal tract would produce in the corresponding configuration. A good model will take account of factors such as limitations in the shapes which can be achieved by the lips, or that the tongue has mass, and therefore cannot move instantaneously from one position to another. In other words, coarticulation effects will be generated automatically, which is the beauty of this approach.

A good model should be based on measurements, which would ideally be taken simultaneously, of all the relevant parameters in a human vocal tract. Obvious limitations exist as to how many instruments can be pushed into and around a person's throat and mouth while he or she speaks, so making the taking of all these measurements simultaneously impossible. Instead the modeller must rely on measurements taken at different times of a person saying the same sounds. Even given such measurements, it is difficult to construct a model which accounts for all the complex interactions between the different components. All the same, good progress is being made in this area, and in the future the best quality text-to-speech synthesizers will be based upon vocal tract models.

We can look forward to the day when users will be able to select and mould voices to their own requirements. It may be that people who know they are going to lose the use of their voice will be able to have a synthetic voice modelled on their own. Alternatively, people may select a voice which they think suits them, rather as they might select a new nose before plastic surgery.

Connections and Compatibility

The technology of speech synthesizers has been described, but a synthesizer must be connected to a computer. The different ways in which this is done need to be explained. Doing so also highlights a recurring problem of current technology – that of compatibility.

All computers have input and output ports through which **peripheral devices** may be connected. Physically a port is just a socket in the computer which will accept a standard plug. The peripheral is connected to the plug through a cable. The common peripherals are items such as printers, but a speech synthesizer may be connected in the same way. Programs which run on the computer can be written so that they send data to an output port and those data are then processed by the peripheral. In the case of a printer that processing takes the form of the data being printed out, whereas a speech synthesizer might be sent the same data, and it would speak them.

The fact that a printer or a synthesizer can be connected to the same port is thanks to the establishment of standards. In particular, there is a standard specification for the electrical connections known as RS232. Additionally, there is the **ASCII** standard format for encoding textual information. Thus, if the description of a speech synthesizer says that it connects via an RS232 port and accepts ASCII input, it implies that it will be compatible with most standard computers.

Most of the electronic components of a computer are fixed to printed circuit boards (also known as cards) which slot into the computer. Another way of connecting a synthesizer is by way of an additional card which fits into a spare slot in the computer. That will be connected by a cable to further external hardware, which may consist simply of a loudspeaker, or may incorporate further speech processing components.

Since the way cards connect together inside the computer varies widely between different computers, synthesizers which connect through a circuit card can generally be connected to only one kind of computer. They are thus much more restrictive than synthesizers which connect through an RS232 port. So, for instance, a card-based synthesizer which works with an IBM **PC** will *not* work with an Apple™ II. On the other hand, both those computers have RS232 ports and so could be connected to any synthesizer with such a connection. That is true of the hardware connections at least. The software must also be available to drive the synthesizer on either computer.

The discussion above introduces an aspect of information technology which is a constant source of frustration and wastage: incompatibility. For economic and technical reasons, it is all too common that items of hardware and software which perform almost identical functions are not interchangeable.

The description of the adaptation of the human–computer interface through the addition of a screen reader, in Chapter 1, was somewhat idealized. At some point every computer user comes across the question of compatibility, or rather the problem of incompatibility. At the most obvious level, there are many computer manufacturers. Each tries to make a product which is better than its rivals' and so sell more of them, so obviously there will be differences between computers manufactured by different companies. In general that means that programs will run on only one range of machines: a program for an Apple II will not run on an IBM PC. Indeed, technological differences usually make software incompatible across different ranges of computers from the same manufacturer: that Apple II program will not run on an Apple Macintosh™ either. This is what you might think of as the first level of incompatibility.

There are commercial reasons which favour perpetuating incompatibility. If manufacturer X manages to convince you that its computer is best for your purposes, it will also want to sell you more equipment and more computers. If you then want a printer, you may well discover that only printers from the same manufacturer will work with your computer. What is more, when you come to buy another computer – either because your business has expanded and you need two of them or because the old one is outdated – all your programs and data will be compatible with that range of machines only, and there you are, tied into it.

The answer to such restrictions is standardization. This has occurred to some extent within the microcomputer market, though not through any externally imposed efforts. IBM developed its PC range of microcomputers, which became very successful. Other manufacturers then began to develop computers which were very similar to the PC, to the extent that they *could* run the same software. These are the PC-compatibles, also referred to sometimes as 'clones' as they are so similar to the original. What is more, most clone manufacturers managed to sell their computers at a lower price than the original. In this way the PC-compatible became firmly established as a *de facto* standard.

However, a problem remains, which George Orwell might have characterized as 'All clones are compatible, but some are more compatible than others.' Compatibility is a relative term. PC-compatibles are not true clones so they do differ from one another and from the original. The differences may show up in one or two particular items of software, which may not run properly on one clone or another. Such incompatibilities are most likely to show up whenever the software does anything unusual – which is just the sort of job expected of adaptations such as screen readers.

The problem of incompatibility extends much further. Often the only sure way to tell whether a particular configuration of hardware and software will work is to try it. For example on might successfully run one word processor with a particular screen reader on one manufacturer's PC, but find the same combination does not run on another computer.

Incompatibilities have also been seen in the domestic market. Some years ago, when video recorders were just becoming cheap enough for general use, there were two formats available: VHS and Betamax. Tapes for a VHS machine would not play on a Betamax and vice versa. Once you had bought a player you were committed to that format and could watch only compatible tapes. For a while both systems were about equally popular and video makers had either to invest in producing two versions of every tape or risk halving their market. The analogy grows tenuous here, since it is a relatively simple matter to copy a video from one format to another, while this is not true of computer programs. Another important difference in this scenario is that the video market eventually settled into stability, VHS emerging as the more popular format, and hence effectively the standard. This is what each of the microcomputer manufacturers would like to happen – as long as *its* computer becomes the standard. Although the IBM PC has become by far the best-selling machine, it has by no means obliterated the opposition.

Dectalk

The history of speech synthesis goes back well beyond the introduction of digital electronic technology. Poulton (1983) includes a brief history of some of the very early attempts to reproduce speech-like sounds. The more recent story of the development of electronic synthesis is contained in Klatt (1987), which includes a gramophone record of samples of the speech produced by different historical synthesizers.

Dennis Klatt was a prominent figure in the modern development of speech synthesis. His work formed the basis of the research synthesizers MITalk and Klattalk. The latter led to the development of the commercial synthesizer, Dectalk. This is thought by many to be the synthesizer which currently produces the best quality speech though it is somewhat expensive. It is manufactured by the Digital Electronic Corporation and, as a commercial product, most of its technical details are confidential. However, the details of its 'cousin' MITalk are thoroughly documented, notably in Allen, Hunnicutt and Klatt (1987). A good description of Dectalk can be found in Bruckert (1984).

The Dectalk can be connected to a computer or terminal through a standard RS232 serial link. One of the intended uses of Dectalk was for sending telephone messages and it therefore also has telephone connections. An important feature of Dectalk is that it offers a range of different voices, both male and female and of different ages, including children. These are identified by friendly names:

1. Paul, an average, middle-aged male;
2. Harry, who sounds taller and heavier than Paul;
3. Frank, who sounds like an older male;
4. Betty, an average, middle-aged woman;
5. Rita, who would be taller and heavier than Betty;
6. Ursula, who sounds younger than Betty;
7. Kit, who is a child who would be about eight years old;
8. Variable Val, a user-definable voice.

The range of voices means that the synthesizer can be programmed to use a different voice when in alternative roles (e.g. one voice when reading computer output from a computer screen and another when echoing the user's typing). Alternatively, it allows the user to select the voice which he or she prefers.

Dectalk is essentially a special purpose computer. It includes the same kind of processor as is found in many modern computers (a Motorola 68000) but, unlike a general purpose computer, it runs only one program. That program is contained in part of its **265 kbytes** of **read-only memory (ROM)**. The text-to-speech conversion is based not on phonemes as such, but on a set of sixty allophones. Input to the software is ASCII text, which is converted by the software into the appropriate allophones. The output also includes embedded control commands.

As described for the general case earlier, Dectalk incorporates an exception dictionary. One of the reasons that the quality of speech of Dectalk is so high is that it has a very large exception dictionary. There are 6,000 entries built in, stored in ROM, comprising:

1. words which are exceptions to the pronunciation rules of English (e.g. bough, though, cough, etc.);
2. words which would be mispronounced if Dectalk's text-to-speech rules were applied;
3. words that are useful to phrase structure for assigning intonation to an utterance without relying solely on punctuation (e.g. 'and' and 'or', which are unstressed

function words, but which might be assigned stress if the default intonation rules were applied);

4. frequently used abbreviations (e.g. Mr, Mrs, Dr).

In addition to the built-in dictionary, there is a user-definable dictionary of 150 entries. This allows users to tailor the speech, usually by adding specialized words relating to their particular application, which are not contained in the built-in dictionary.

The average active working vocabulary of a graduate is estimated to be 15,000 words. Having such large dictionaries thus implies that there is a high probability of any word to be spoken being in the dictionary, but those which are not in either of the dictionaries are passed on to the letter-to-sound rules. These specify not only the pronunciation, but also their syllable and stress patterns. Again, the high quality of the speech is partly due to the extensive set of rules applied at this stage.

This first stage of processing deals with the pronunciation of individual words. Its output is passed on to the second stage, which deals with variations in pronunciation signalled by the punctuation and due to coarticulation effects of adjacent words. There are a number of voice parameters which can be altered in Dectalk. It is by appropriate selection of these parameters that the variety of voices mentioned earlier is achieved. They include:

- smoothness;
- head size;
- voice forte;
- breathiness;
- creakiness.

Smoothness controls the voicing energy at high frequencies. Head size is an important characteristic, which is one of the main variations between the adult voices and that of Kit, the child. Forte dictates how well the voice will carry. Its maximum setting of 100 would be used to make a voice which carries well in a noisy environment, while its minimum setting of 0 is much softer, and is even claimed to be 'sexy'. Breathiness can be set in the range 0 (no breathiness) to 40 (a strong breath noise). Creakiness controls the occurrence of irregular voicing pulses at the beginnings and ends of sentences, and can range from 0 to 100. The characteristics must be altered together to get a pleasant, human-sounding voice. For instance, if one increases the breathiness it is generally necessary also to increase the smoothness.

In addition to these voice parameters, commands are also available to control other suprasegmental features, such as tone, pauses and intonation.

Once the stream of allophones and commands has been generated, it is passed on to the voice-generation stage. This is based upon a digital signal processor which generates the voice waveform by sending pitch pulses through a series of resonators. The output of the resonators is essentially a digitized waveform of a form similar to that described above (see the discussion on digitization in Speech synthesis, above) which is then passed to a digital-to-analogue converter to produce the final output through the speaker.

The first production Dectalk was released in 1983. In 1985 an improved version was released which was smaller, as well as incorporating improvements to speech quality. The newer version is available as a plug-in card, but the connection for both versions is through an RS232 serial port.

Further Reading

Rowden (1986) discusses some of the disadvantages of using synthetic speech in communication aids.

Isard and Miller (1986) discuss diphone synthesis techniques.

Those interested in more details of techniques of compressing digitized speech through linear predictive coding can refer to Tremain (1982), Atal and Hanauer (1971), Schroeder (1985) and Atal and Schroeder (1970).

Newell (1986) discusses many of the issues of the use of speech synthesis by disabled people.

This chapter included a discussion of the quality of synthetic speech. Although it is generally agreed that there is plenty of scope for improvement, research is proceeding as to how it might be taken to the stage of being able to express emotions. This is reported in Murray, Arnott and Newell (1988).

3 Human–Computer Interaction

The Human–Computer Interface

This chapter introduces human–computer interaction as a discipline which is the study of the way in which people interact with computers – and other information technology machines. It is a relatively new area of investigation and up to now has been largely concerned with what might be described as the *average* computer **user**. The needs of exceptional users, those with disabilities, have hitherto been treated as a specialization, outside human–computer interaction. However, it is coming to be recognized that the study of the particular needs of people who are disabled is just as much a valid part of human–computer interaction as (say) the special needs of novice computer users. As part of that trend, this chapter describes the position of the subject matter of this book within the discipline of human–computer interaction.

A computer is an information-processing machine. It must interact with the environment in which it operates. In its simplest terms it receives input information which it can store and transform and, as and when appropriate, it communicates information back to the world around it. In general the computer must communicate with people. This communication may be more or less direct. For instance, a **word processor** is a highly interactive program, which relies on a person to input information on a keyboard directly, and it is people who will read the text eventually printed out by the program. Other computers work rather more autonomously, but even the most highly automated process control will be monitored by people – because we cannot trust the computer and its programs completely.

There is a fundamental mismatch between computers and people. Computers are unintelligent and cannot communicate in the same ways as people do. Being unintelligent, they are also unadaptable and so it is generally the person who has to find ways of communicating which suit the computer, rather than the other way around.

The mediator of communication between people and computers is variously referred to as the human–computer interface (HCI), the human–machine interface (HMI) or the man–machine interface (MMI). Communication is two-way. Information passing from the person to the computer is usually described as *input*, while communication in the other direction is *output*. Despite the potential confusion, these words are also often used as verbs.

Early computer systems relied almost entirely on the adaptability of the user to bridge the gap of the human–computer interface. It was up to the user to determine how the computer worked and what was expected of the user. Since the computer had been designed and built by other people it was perfectly feasible to find out about its interface. The user could be supplied with diagrams and written descriptions of the behaviour of the machine. However, though it was feasible to understand the computer in these terms, it was difficult and was possible only for individuals with appropriate ability and training – similar to that of the people who had built the computer. This was not a problem when computers were few in number and limited in their application; only a small number needed to use them and so people with the appropriate abilities could be found.

As with so many aspects of computing, a major change occurred with the introduction of the **microprocessor**. Computers became so cheap that it was possible to use them in a much wider range of applications. Indeed, manufacturing costs can be kept low only if large volumes are produced, so that new markets had to be created to generate demand. Larger markets mean that more people will use computers, but they cannot all be highly trained. Hence computers had to be made such that they can be used with as little training as possible.

The major influence on ease of use is the human–computer interface. A completely new field of research into human–computer interaction has developed, largely concerned with investigating what the factors are which influence the quality of an interface, and hence how computer systems can be made easier to use. No longer is it possible to expect that all users would have an intimate understanding of the way the computer works; instead the computer system has to be designed so that it is matched and adapted to the user. The problem is that whereas the user can obtain diagrams and descriptions of precisely how the computer works, plans of the human mind are not available! The psychologist or HCI designer cannot 'take the lid off' the user's mind, but can only study the external manifestations of the user's behaviour.

The physical sciences are based on laws, which are well established, unvarying descriptions of how things work in the real world. Perhaps the best-known such law is Newton's law of gravity. This states that all objects are attracted to one another, which is why an apple falls towards the earth.[1] Furthermore, such laws enable the physicist to predict measurable quantities, such as the speed the apple will be moving at when it hits the ground. Other branches of science do not have such laws, because the scientists have not yet been able to sort out the complexity of the phenomena they observe. In such circumstances they often apply *models* instead of laws.

For instance, the human mind is so complex that there are no complete theories of how it works. However, it is possible to devise models which describe certain forms of behaviour, possibly within restrictive constraints. Such a model can be used as the basis of experiments. If the model is a good one, the results of experiments will reflect the behaviour to be expected of the represented system. In reality most models are incomplete, and therefore are sometimes but not always good representations. An

---

[1] Strictly speaking, the law of gravity states that the apple is attracted to the earth, but the earth is also attracted to the apple, so that the apple not only falls towards the earth, but the earth also moves up to meet it. The difference is that the earth is so huge that its movement is not detectable.

important feature of all models is that they give a measure of *predictability*. Questions of how the system can be expected to react in given circumstances can be answered by applying the same parameters to its model and seeing how it reacts.

Physical models are used in engineering. For instance, in developing racing yachts, scale models are built and tested in water tanks. A model costs a lot less to build than a full-size craft so that the designer can afford to experiment with different designs and configurations, and essentially perform 'What if . . .' experiments, such as 'If the ratio of length to beam is increased will the boat go faster?'

A map may also be considered to be a model. It is possible to perform experiments along the lines of 'What happens if I turn left at the church?' A map may be an incomplete model: mistakes may have been made in drawing it, or it may not have been updated to keep up with changes in the landscape. It is possible to internalize maps, as mental models. Often we build up mental maps by exploring an area. However, if we want to find our way around an unfamiliar area quickly we may make use of a model provided for us, in the form of a printed map.

Three models are of importance to human–computer interface designers:

1. the user's model of the computer;
2. the computer's model of the user; and
3. the designer's model of the user.

The user's model of the computer is a mental model. Use of the computer can be facilitated if the interface embodies an explicit and well-designed model which explains the computer's behaviour in a way which is consistent with the user's experience of the (non-computer) world. For long enough the only model of the computer was a description of how it worked at the level of operations on numbers. Since computers are very complex and work on the basis of logic such models were completely inaccessible to most (untrained) people.

It was with the development of the Xerox Star computer that designers began to think about providing the user with a more accessible model. Such interfaces draw heavily on analogy, and the most popular analogy is the desk top. The interface consists of a screen which displays visual representations of components such as documents, folders and filing cabinets – items already familiar to most users. Users manipulate these items in a manner similar to the way they would handle their real-world counterparts. So, for example, they can effectively pick up a document and put it into a folder, and the folder can be put into a filing cabinet. In fact what the user does is to 'point' at pictures resembling documents, folders and filing cabinets. The pointing is carried out through a **mouse**, which was another innovation in the Star interface. A mouse is a box which fits into the palm of the hand and lies on a flat surface, such as a desk. The mouse is physically attached to the computer and connected to a pointer item on the screen, called the 'cursor'. As the mouse is moved around the cursor also moves correspondingly, so that if the mouse is moved to the right, the cursor also moves that way. Pushing the mouse away causes the cursor to move upwards, and so on. So, for example, to put a document in a folder, the user might point the cursor at a picture (or 'icon') representing the document, press a button on the mouse and then move the mouse to point the cursor at an icon representing the folder. As the mouse moves the document icon follows it, and it can then be 'dropped' into the folder by releasing the mouse button (see Figure 3.1).

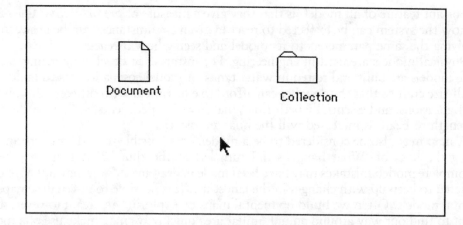

Figure 3.1   Icons in a graphical user interface. The Document icon, on the left, represents a file, while the Collection icon, on the right, represents a folder, which can contain a number of files. The arrow is the cursor.

The desk top provides users with a readily understandable model of what goes on inside the computer – which has nothing to do with numbers and electronic circuits (at least not directly). Once the user has learned a few simple conventions, such as how to point at an item and the effects of the mouse button, he or she can generally use the computer with minimal assistance. When users encounter problems they will be able to tackle them by making predictions based on the model (i.e. what would happen on a real desk), supplemented with their knowledge of the conventions of the interface. So, interfaces are now constructed which embody an explicit model the user can apply to understand the behaviour of the computer.

Taking the second kind of model, building a model of the user into the computer interface means that the interface can be more adaptable to individuals. Such an interface will be more intelligent and hence can relieve users of some of their workload. However, users are people and therefore varied and complex, and it is very difficult to construct such a model (or models). As mentioned earlier, an important use of models is in prediction. A good user model should enable the computer to anticipate the user's behaviour. Very few computers (as yet) include a model of the user, and hence interactions with computers can be quite inefficient and stilted.

Designers will be able to produce a good interface only if they have an accurate picture of the likely users – a good model of them. In other words, designers must have some kind of specification or image of the skills and other characteristics of the likely average users of the system. That model may be quite explicit, based on research and experiments, but more often than not it is rather more implicit, and based on the designer's own ideas and introspection.

One of the problems of designing good human–computer interfaces mentioned above was the lack of any 'blueprints' of the human mind. If any such blueprints – or even approximations to them – are to be found, we would expect them to emerge from the discipline of psychology, and indeed psychology does provide some important contributions to the study of human–computer interaction.

One approach is to take an established principle of human psychology and see what its implications are for a person using a computer. An example is Fitts's law of pointing, which was devised in the 1950s when computers were so crude and rare that the concept of there being interactions between them and humans was hardly even recognized. Nevertheless this law is entirely applicable to modern human–computer interactions using a mouse. The law states how long it will take a person to point at a target of a given size from a given starting point. That time is:

$$T_{position} = I_M \log_2 (2D/s)$$

Where: I_M is a constant
D is the (linear) distance to the target
s is the size of the target (Fitts, 1954).

Fitts's law has been applied within the development of human–computer interfaces to make predictions about performance on tasks and to experiment with proposed interface designs before they are actually implemented (Roberts and Moran, 1982; Card, Moran and Newell, 1983).

Pointing behaviour, as described by Fitts's law, is very simple. Unfortunately there are not many such clear-cut, simple psychological principles and none which accurately describes more complex behaviour. Another psychological approach to human–computer interaction therefore is not based on established principles, but relies on experiments which measure people's interactions with specific aspects of the interface and then sees if principles can be extracted which can then be applied to improve design. For example, the Keystroke-Level Model (Card, Moran and Newell, 1980, 1983) provides a means for predicting how long it will take a person to perform interactive tasks. The model is derived from analysis of the tasks and filled out with numbers which are ascertained by experimental measurements.

Notice the difference which is implied by the fact that Fitts's description of pointing behaviour is described as a *law*, while other approaches are based on *models* – such as the Keystroke Model. A law is something with universal applicability while a model is less general. There is no inherent reason why a given person should type in the manner predicted by the Keystroke-Level Model. Indeed it is easy to find exceptions, such as novice 'hunt and peck', one-finger typists. Models – of greater or lesser validity – are easier to devise when one is dealing with human behaviour. Similarly, when drawing conclusions from psychological investigations of human–computer interaction, it is often more profitable not to attempt to devise rules governing how interfaces ought to be implemented. Instead one is more likely to make suggestions, in the form of guidelines. See, for instance, Smith and Mosier (1986).

One feature of nearly all designers' models of users is the assumption that the user has average physical and sensory abilities; most human–computer interfaces are not designed to be used by people with disabilities.

This book is concerned with interfaces which *have* been designed with the needs of disabled users in mind. Some of the devices studied have been developed especially for use by people with specific disabilities. The others are adaptive devices intended to overcome the inaccessibility of certain interfaces to certain users. An example of the former would be a reading machine, the function of which is to read books to blind people. Since this is specifically intended for use by blind people it had to be designed in such a way as to make it as easy as possible for them to use. An example of the latter is a screen reader, which is a means of making the text on a computer screen accessible to a blind user by translating its contents into synthetic speech.

In pointing out that designers tend to neglect the needs of disabled users there is no intention to imply that all interfaces should be designed to be accessible to all people, regardless of disability. Such a suggestion would be ridiculous; for example, an interface which relies on auditory information and which is thus accessible to a blind user would be inaccessible to a deaf person. It is natural that designers of any product will aim it at what is envisaged as the average potential user, for there lies the maximum potential market. There are two points to be made, though. One is that the design of interfaces for people with special requirements because of disabilities should be treated in the same way as the design of other interfaces; it should become a part of the discipline of human–computer interaction. Second, if at least some consideration were paid to the likely needs of disabled users early in the design process, better and more easily adapted interfaces should result.

Progress has already been made in these directions. Conferences and journals in the field of human–computer interaction do regularly feature work on specialized interfaces for disabled users. Also, legislation in the United States has forced computer manufacturers to consider the needs of disabled users. Section 508 of the Rehabilitation Amendments Act 1986 requires that office automation products purchased or rented by government units must conform to a set of guidelines regarding accessibility to disabled people. This is a significant piece of legislation which is likely to have far-reaching effects. The US government is the largest buyer of computer equipment in the world, so manufacturers ignore its requirements at their peril. In fact, all the major manufacturers have been very responsive, setting up a working group which has investigated how the legislation requirements should be met. The effect will also spread because no manufacturer is likely to build two models of a computer – one which conforms to the government's requirements and one for sale to other customers. This also means that designers will think about the needs of disabled users much earlier in the design process. Adaptations will become not so much add-on components which have to be bolted on awkwardly within constraints imposed by the standard interface, but should fit on smoothly, as a matter of course.

The legislation is not prescriptive. It does not attempt to force manufacturers to make particular modifications to their products, but rather encourages them to devise means of giving access to the equipment to people with a whole range of disabilities.

> The disabled end user shall have access to the same data bases, operating, and application programs; shall be equipped with adaptive programs and devices to support his or her disabilities; shall have computing capability not appreciably less than that of non-disabled end users in the same position and office; and shall be supported in manipulating data so as to attain end results equivalent to the non-disabled user.
>
> (Gray *et al.*, 1987, p. 1)

Further details of this legislation will also be found in Scadden and Vanderheiden (1988).

Computer screens are becoming increasingly complex. If the designer needs to communicate another piece of information to the user, he or she can simply add an additional visual indicator on the screen and rely on the power and flexibility of vision to cope with the extra complexity. There is a suggestion, though, that visual displays are approaching a state of 'visual overload'. With a better understanding of non-visual communication it may be possible to use a different medium to communicate the additional information and so reduce this load. Similarly, novel forms of interaction may need to be devised so that a physically disabled person can interact with a computer-based device, and the lessons learned in developing such interactions may have a broader significance in helping more physically able users to tackle ever more complex tasks through computers.

The ultimate aim of most technological aids for disabled people is to increase the independence of the user. The designer of any human–machine interface intended for use by disabled people must be very much aware of this. For instance, a communication device which can be used by a physically disabled person but which has an on–off switch that can be operated only by someone with good manual dexterity does not give the user the degree of independence which it might: the user will still be under the control of other people who can decide when the device will and will not be available.

Interface Requirements of Blind Users

'Visual disability' is a generic term which covers a whole range of sight impairments. As stated earlier, the vast majority of visually disabled people do have some sight. This section is concerned with people with no sight at all, whose needs are very different from those of partially sighted people. The partially sighted need the opportunity to make maximum use of their residual vision. They need aids which boost that sight, such as magnifiers and special lighting. Such people generally resist using devices which have been designed for blind users and which have no provision for them to use their sight.

In designing any product to be used by people who are blind, however, one must communicate via the non-visual senses. The obvious ones are hearing and touch, although, as will be seen below, we should not forget others such as touch and the kinaesthetic sense (which is the information we get from our muscles so that we know where our arm is in space even with our eyes closed). Braille is an example of adapting visual communication (print) to a tactile form, accessible to blind people. It is not, however, as useful a medium as is often assumed. The major disadvantage of braille is that the vast majority of blind people cannot read it. There are various reasons for this, but they amount to the fact that most individuals find it too difficult to learn. This is exacerbated by the fact that the onset of visual degeneration is often accompanied by a decrease in tactile sensitivity.

For those who can read it, braille output can be provided from computers, but there are further practical problems. A number of braille embossers, which are essentially printers which produce braille on paper instead of print from a computer, are available. These are expensive, slow and noisy, but as a means of producing paper braille are invaluable. Braille embossed by a computer on to paper is to the blind computer user as a print-out is to the sighted user: it is permanent; large amounts are accessible (i.e. more than one screenful) but it is bulky.

Information on a screen is much more transient and controllable and blind users also need the same kind of access. This can be provided on what are known as *soft* braille displays. These are the braille equivalents of the computer visual display screen – the contents of which can change rapidly and frequently. The basic problem with soft braille displays is that they are mechanical devices, composed of rods, springs and electromagnets. Compared to the chips of computers (with no moving parts) such devices have a very low level of reliability. The more components in a mechanical device, the greater its potential for failure. A single braille cell consists of six dots, implying there must be six sets of components, which must all be of a suitably miniature size. An eighty-cell display has 480 dots or pins and any one of them failing or sticking can make the output very difficult to read properly. At the same time, it is very expensive to manufacture these small mechanical components with sufficient precision.

Existing braille displays usually consist of a relatively small number of cells. An obvious extension of the idea would be to develop a whole-screen braille display. However, the problems mentioned above are multiplied. No such displays have yet been practically implemented, though much work is continuing on their development. Another common idea still being investigated is that of a braille mouse. The basic idea is to have a mouse attached to a computer in the normal way but on the mouse is a single soft braille cell (or two or three of them). If the cursor is moved over text on the screen, it is reproduced in braille on the mouse. Again there are a number of problems with this idea, such that currently it remains in the realms of research alone.

Many of the problems of adapting the human–computer interface for use by blind people arise from the fundamental differences between sight and the other senses. The fact that more information can be presented visually at one time was discussed in Chapter 1. This is because it is possible to switch visual attention very quickly between different sources of information. Although it has been argued that hearing does have more of an ability to receive parallel information than is often realized, it is still true that such large amounts of information cannot be presented simultaneously in an auditory or a tactile form. This generally implies that there is a much greater load on the memory of the user of an adapted interface. For example, screens often include an area which displays helpful prompts to the user. These may be reminders of the commands available and the keystrokes associated with them. To refer to these the user merely needs to glance at that part of the screen. There is no real equivalent of a glance for the user of an adapted (auditory or braille) screen. To shift attention to a different part of the screen is generally a significant activity, so that it is much easier if the user can *remember* all the commands.

Listening to text is different from reading it visually in that it is much more difficult to detect spelling errors. Often words can be misspelt in such a way that it is not possible to hear the error. Also, the quality of pronunciation of some synthesizers is such that the synthesizer may be blamed for a word sounding wrong. Proofreading can be difficult and tedious. Hearing a document spoken by a synthetic voice can be tedious and hard to follow, but hearing it spoken letter by letter is out of the question. In word processing it is therefore imperative that good quality spelling checkers must be available. It is still often necessary to examine words letter by letter, but just as it is sometimes difficult to distinguish similar sounding words, the pronunciation of some letters can be confusing (B and P, for instance). A useful feature, therefore, is the option of having letters spoken in a phonetic alphabet, such as that used in radio communications (Alpha, Bravo, Charlie, etc.).

The screen reader, being an adaptation, involves two interfaces. There is the interface designed to mediate between the computer and a sighted user. To create an interface

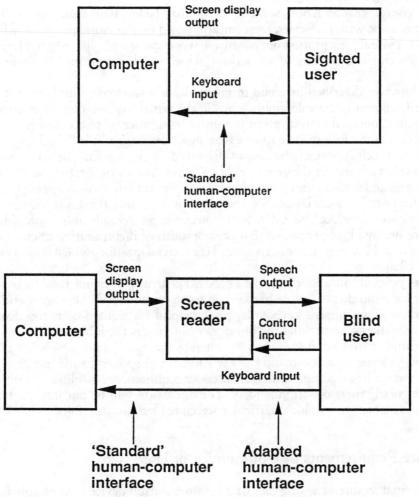

Figure 3.2 A screen reader adapts the human–computer interface. On the left, it effectively intercepts the standard interface, transforming it such that it is accessible to blind users.

between the computer and a blind user there must be interposed the adaptation, which on one side effectively has the same interface to the computer as the sighted user, but transforms that on the other side into a form accessible to the blind user. Figure 3.2 illustrates how the screen reader resolves the mismatch between the standard visual human–computer interface and the blind user.

Notice that the keyboard interface to the computer is unchanged. This is because blind people generally can learn to touch-type so that no adaptation is necessary. An additional input channel has been added, through which the user can control the screen reader. The interaction between this control input and the speech which is output constitutes the adapted human–computer interface which should be tailored to the needs and skills of a blind user.

Adapting a visual interface in this way imposes certain constraints on the resultant human–computer interaction, some of which may be less than desirable. For instance, the user is stuck with the screen representation used by the visual program, which may be ideal for visual presentation but confusing when translated into speech. Nevertheless, this approach has a number of attractions, which are discussed more fully in Chapter 4.

The interface described here and in Figure 3.2 is a relatively simple one: it assumes that the keyboard is the sole input device in the visual human–computer interface. In fact the most noticeable innovation in human–computer interaction in recent years is the addition of the mouse. The mouse is an input device, but it is linked very closely to the cursor, which is part of the *output* displayed on the screen. The term 'wimp' has been coined as a name for the interfaces of systems which incorporate a mouse: window, icon, mouse and pull-down menu. However, more recently writers appear to prefer to avoid the negative associations of the word wimp, and the more current term is 'graphical user interface', or GUI. Such interfaces are considerably more difficult to adapt for use by blind people, so that the approach of incorporating a screen reader is not sufficient. However, there is a real need for such adaptation, which is discussed more fully in Chapter 5.

It was pointed out above that the keyboard generally does not have to be specially adapted for blind users. Tactile markers on some of the 'home' keys are useful and are standard on many current keyboards, being helpful for sighted users too. Even given these tactile marks, something the blind user can miss is the labels on the keys. A very useful feature, therefore, is some facility whereby the user can press a key but instead of generating a letter or a command the key's identity is spoken to the user.

This section has examined the user interface requirements of blind computer users, and particularly users of screen readers. The discussion will be put into context more clearly in Chapter 4, in which particular screen readers are examined.

Interface Requirements of Communicator Users

The principal requirement of a user of a communication device is to be able to specify and produce speech at a very fast rate. Normal conversation proceeds at a rate of around 150 words per minute, so ideally someone who uses a communicator as his or her voice in a conversation should be able to generate speech at that rate. However, that is very difficult to attain. The only existing input systems which are capable of attaining such speeds are stenotypes, which are described later in this section.

In this section several different input techniques are described which attempt to optimize the conflicting requirements of rapid input with limited dexterity. Most of the devices have common features, which can best be explained as variations on the basic idea of a keyboard. At the most general level, inputting information into a computer entails communicating selections from a vocabulary known to the computer and stringing them together into messages. In the case of the conventional keyboard the vocabulary is the letters, numbers and punctuation marks of the language. These can be used to build arbitrary utterances. Selection is based on two-dimensional space. There are two stages to selection: location of the appropriate key followed by the commitment implied by pressing that key.

Other input devices all share these features: a *vocabulary* and selection based on *location* and *commitment* actions. Input can be accelerated in two ways: by reducing the number of selection events per utterance and by reducing the time taken to perform each selection event. The number of selection events can be reduced by increasing the vocabulary or, in other words, increasing the number of keys. There is a limit to the effectiveness of doing this, though, because the size of the keyboard would reach such proportions that the location time would increase: physically to move a finger to a key would take an appreciable time and it would become very hard to remember the location of each key. On conventional keyboards the shift key provides a mechanism whereby the number of characters accessible is doubled by the addition of a single key.[1] The character produced when the user presses any key depends on whether the shift key is down or not. If the key is a letter key it will be in upper case if the shift is down, for instance.

The technical term for such a technique is that the keyboard is *modal*. That means that the effect of pressing any key is not always the same, but depends on the current mode of the keyboard. For a typewriter keyboard there are just two modes: shifted and unshifted. The same technique can be extended so that a keyboard may have several modes, and an example of this is the Touch Talker™, described in Chapter 4.

For people who lack the manual dexterity to use a conventional keyboard there are other letter-selection devices. In general they operate by substituting temporal discrimination for spatial discrimination. The simplest example would be to have all the letters of the alphabet displayed on a screen and each one highlighted in turn. When the required letter is highlighted the user would activate a switch. Given the number of letters in the alphabet and the limitations of reaction times, location times would be very slow and the overall speed would be very low, since the input unit is the letter and there are a large number of letters in the average utterance.

Another way of speeding up input rates is to reduce the time to locate each input token. To this end there are a number of variations on the use of grids (or 'matrices') for letter selection. One version is illustrated in Figure 3.3. A letter is selected in two stages, corresponding to its row and column in the matrix. Each row of the matrix is highlighted in turn and when the row containing the required letter is highlighted a switch is pressed. That causes each of the letters in that row to be highlighted and the desired one can be selected by pressing the switch when it is highlighted.

The switches referred to above can take many forms and are generally tailored to the abilities of individual users. If a user does not have sufficient control to operate a hand switch some other part of the body will be used: the foot, the head, the chin – any part over which the user has sufficient voluntary control. A user who cannot make movements as such might use a mouth switch operated by breath control. If a user has sufficient control and co-ordination he or she may use more than one switch, and so speed up input. For instance, someone who can use two switches may use one to control the horizontal scanning of a letter matrix, and the other to control the vertical scanning.

It has to be said that the letter-based input described above is generally the slowest form. Its only real advantage is that it does mean that the user can generate arbitrary utterances. In other words, if the input is based upon letter selection any utterance in the

---

[1] Actually three keys on most keyboards: two shift keys and a shift-lock, but in principle the same effect could be realized by a single shift key.

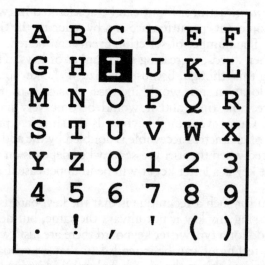

Figure 3.3 *A matrix of letters which might be used as the basis of an input device. The letters are scanned by a cursor and can be selected by pressing a switch when the appropriate letter is indicated. In the diagram the letter I is currently selected. A variety of scanning strategies and different numbers of switches can be used.*

language can be constructed. However, given that the average English word has six letters, it will take six selections per word. (The relationship between generality and speed of input with different levels of input units is illustrated in Figure 3.4.) Letter-based input is accessible to people with even the most severe physical impairments, through the sort of simple switch system described. However, as will be seen below, such switches can also be used with other, higher-level input devices. Typewriter-style keyboards are used on a number of communication devices, but the other letter-selection techniques are generally too slow for use in communication devices, and are more commonly used as a means of adapting computers for physically disabled users.

Another way of increasing the input rate of communication is to take the elements

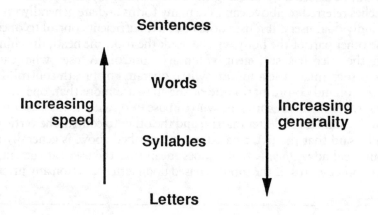

Figure 3.4 *Levels of input selection. The higher the level the faster the input, but the less general utterances that can be generated.*

of the vocabulary from a higher level. For instance, if the vocabulary is words (and given an average word-length of six letters) there is in principle a sixfold increase in input rate. Of course, it is not as simple as that. The advantage of letter-based input is that from a keyboard (of around fifty keys) it is possible to construct any utterance in the language. That would not be possible for word-based input. Any device based solely on word selection can provide only a predefined sub-set of the words of the language. If one were to have a keyboard with one key per word, and a vocabulary of several hundred words, it would be a vast size, which would greatly increase the key location time. However, even for relatively limited vocabularies of a few hundred words special techniques have to be applied to make them accessible from a keyboard of reasonable size. Examples of these techniques are discussed in Chapter 4.

Another problem is that words are used in different forms, with different spellings, within sentences. For instance, it would be undesirable to have to store all conjugations of each verb ('I go', 'she goes', etc.). Two approaches are possible here: to allow users to access the basic words easily, which they can modify as necessary (i.e. the user selects 'go' and then adds 'es'); and to make the system automatically select the correct form of words, depending on their use within the utterance. In practice a combination of these two approaches may be used. Only the user will know if a subject should be in the plural, but having signalled that it is plural, the system might correct the part of the verb used. For instance if the user has selected 'The bird' and then selects the verb 'to fly', the device automatically generates, 'The bird flies', whereas if the user has selected 'The birds', selecting the same verb will cause the utterance to be generated as 'The birds fly'.

Input times can be reduced still further if the user does not have to select every word from the whole vocabulary but from a small sub-set of the vocabulary. Having selected a word, the user can be presented with (say) the six words which are most likely to follow that one. If one of the predictions is correct the user should be able to select the word by a simple one-out-of-six choice, instead of one from 3,000. In this way the computer can be made to take on more of the work by generating the predictions. Ideally this should be based on a dynamic analysis of the user's style of writing and normal selection of words. Among the devices which employ this approach are the Equalizer (Chapter 4) and Pal (Chapter 6).

An input unit which comes somewhere between the letter and the word is the syllable (roughly equivalent to the phoneme). This does represent a compromise between the two. The average word consists of around two syllables, and it is possible to generate all the words of the language from approximately fifty syllables. So input is speeded up by virtue of the fact that it takes on average just two selection events to input one word.

Machines which are based on syllable input are generally called *stenotypes*, which is a generic term covering machines such as the British Palantype and the American Stenograph. These are commonly used in courtrooms as a means of making a verbatim record of the proceedings. As well as using these larger input units, input is also accelerated by minimizing the time taken to make a selection. A stenotype keyboard does not consist of one key per syllable, but has around thirty keys (different machines vary). The larger number of syllables are accessible by use of key *chords* – more than one key pressed simultaneously. Location times are small because all the keys are within easy reach of the fingers. The output from a stenotype is not plain English text, but a shorthand which can be read only by a trained operator. There are computer programs which will translate stenotype input into a more readable form (though still not plain

English) and these are used mainly as **real-time** transcription machines for deaf people.

Stenotypes can be operated only by skilled personnel with a high degree of manual dexterity and are mentioned here only as the ultimate available high-speed keyboard. They are not advocated as an input device for communication device users since the vast majority of such people could never be expected to attain the necessary level of skill to use such a keyboard, especially as many of them have physical impairments which affect their dexterity.

Going one stage higher in the levels of input units, input can be based on complete utterances. This is the fastest form of input in terms of words per selection event, and hence words per second, but it is also the least general form of input, as illustrated in Figure 3.4. In effect the user is confined to speaking only pre-stored utterances.

Some such devices do allow the user to specify the phrases to be stored. Also, there is often the facility to resort to letter-based input if the user needs to say something which has not been pre-stored. Other devices (such as the Claudius Converse – see Appendix A) are somewhat more prescriptive in that all of their utterances are pre-programmed by the manufacturer, but do at least allow the user to specify some personal utterances which are programmed into the machine before delivery to the individual.

The Equalizer has already been referred to in the context of word level input, but in fact it also has facilities for accessing complete utterances, as described in Chapter 4. Researchers at Dundee University are working on the problem of producing conversational speech at high speed by generating sentence-level utterances. This is achieved effectively by making the selection at an even higher level. The aim is to maximize the rate of speech production and to minimize the amount of silence within a conversation. Extended non-participation by one of the people ruins the flow of a conversation and is interpreted as reflecting disagreement or discomfort. The Dundee group has developed a prototype communication device, called Chat, based on a portable PC computer and a speech synthesizer. Chat works on the principle of giving the speed of output a higher priority than precise control over every aspect of what is said.

It was suggested above that Chat's speech production is at the sentence level. This is not strictly true, in a very important way. A vital component of natural conversation is feedback remarks – short utterances made by the listener which encourage the speaker and maintain the listener as an active participant in the interaction. Examples of feedback remarks are:

- *Acknowledge*
  Uh-huh.
  I see.
  Well well.
- *Agree*
  Yes.
  I'm with you on that.
- *Evaluate good*
  That's really good.
  Oh, good.

An appropriate feedback remark can be generated at a single keystroke. They are

Y Yes	**6 Evaluate bad**	**N No**
1 Acknowledge	**7 Repeat request**	**8 Request more info**
2 Agree		
3 Disagree		
4 Don't know		**W Go to wrap up remark**
5 Evaluate good	**9 Filler phrase**	**M Go back to main menu**

Figure 3.5   Chat's menu from which feedback remarks can be generated. Having selected a category (by a single keystroke, 1–9, W, Y, N or M) Chat randomly generates a suitable utterance.

selected from a menu, as shown in Figure 3.5. It would be wearing and unnatural for the same feedback remark to be used in any given situation, hence a number will be built in under each heading, as above. These are not generated in sequence, however, which would be similarly contrived and tedious, but are selected at random. This use of randomness exemplifies the transfer of control of the speech content in favour of increased speed. A particular type of feedback remark is the *filler*. Fillers are the noises and utterances the listener may make which contains no information as such ('um' or 'er', for instance) but nevertheless are an important component of any conversation. Fillers may be used to forestall an interruption, while the speaker is formulating the next utterance, or to signal continuing participation in the conversation.

Another important factor in forming a bond between the participants is the use of names. Chat includes a facility whereby users can store the names of the people they know, which the system will automatically insert at appropriate points in the conversation.

Another important variable in any conversation is the mood or attitude of the speaker, to the person being addressed. Mood is therefore another choice which Chat users make. Figure 3.6 shows the main Chat control screen through which the user can control all the settings mentioned above. Chat conversations are based on the idea that conversations generally follow a very similar pattern: greetings, smalltalk, main section, wrap-up remarks, farewells. Users navigate through these phases of the conversation using the controls in the main control screen. The central box on the main control screen shows Chat's prediction as to the next move in the conversation. If it is correct, the user selects 1: 'Speak and move on'. A suitable utterance is generated and Chat moves on to predict the next phase. If users wish to say something but not to move on (such as when saying goodbye to a number of people) they would select 2. At any time they can also override the predicted flow and go directly to any of the conversational phases.

At this comparatively early stage in their research the Dundee researchers are looking only at the simplest kind of conversation, in which the main section is omitted. That

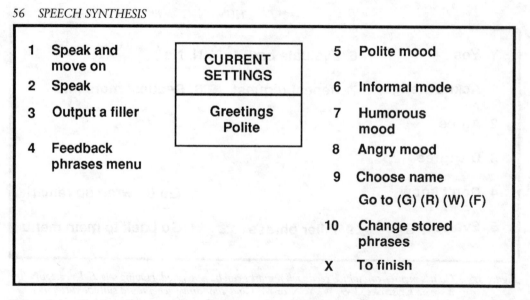

1	Speak and move on	CURRENT SETTINGS	5	Polite mood
2	Speak		6	Informal mode
3	Output a filler	Greetings Polite	7	Humorous mood
4	Feedback phrases menu		8	Angry mood
			9	Choose name
				Go to (G) (R) (W) (F)
			10	Change stored phrases
			X	To finish

Figure 3.6   Chat's main control screen. The user directs the flow of conversation through this menu.

is the sort of conversation one might have with a colleague in a corridor. It is relatively content-free; there is not a vital requirement to communicate specific information.

It has been said that a conversation is a dialogue in which the one taking breath is called the listener. This is not true of conversations in which one of the participants uses a communication device on which it takes much longer than an inhalation to compose and generate an utterance, but ultimately the aim must be to alter that situation so that communication device users can take an equal part in any communication.

The descriptions given above have all been based on the use of a keyboard. In fact the keyboard is being used as a paradigm and can be realized in many forms, some quite unlike a typewriter keyboard. The essential properties which the keyboard paradigm embodies are a two-dimensional array of keys and the facility to activate any one of those keys.

A wide variety of keyboards are used in communication aids which are very different in design, yet equivalent functionally. Such a variety is used because the potential users have a broad range of physical abilities. It has already been mentioned that many users of communication aids cannot exploit the speed of stenotype keyboards because they do not have sufficient manual dexterity. In fact many of them are unable to make use even of the simpler conventional keyboard.

People with physical disabilities can have a number of problems with conventional keyboards. Many people may have problems with the basic action of pressing a key. For a start, it should not be assumed that users will necessarily be pressing the keys with their fingers. They may well use a stick attached to some part of their body such as their head. The part of the body used to press keys (be it hand, head or whatever) will be selected as one over which the person has good control, but nevertheless there will be limitations on that control.

On most computer keyboards key pressing can be a three-stage process, as illustrated in Figure 3.7. The user first locates and presses the key. It must be held down for a

User locates the
key

User presses
the key

Single character
generated:

k

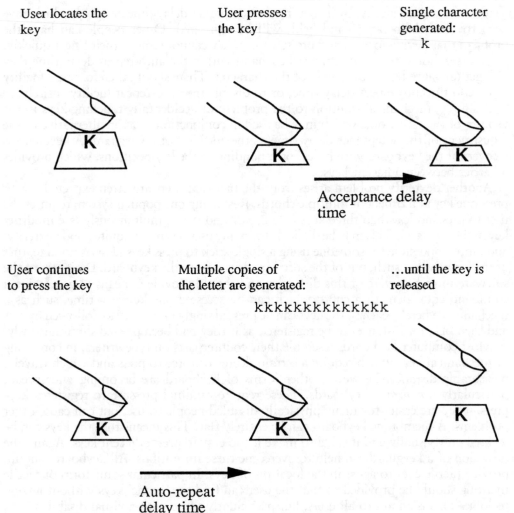

Acceptance delay
time

User continues
to press the key

Multiple copies of
the letter are generated:

...until the key is
released

kkkkkkkkkkkkk

Auto-repeat
delay time

*Figure 3.7   Pressing a key on a computer keyboard is in fact a three-stage process. Pressing the key
generates one letter. Then holding it down for longer than the acceptance delay time will
cause copies of the letter to be generated.*

certain time before it is registered as having been pressed, so effectively nothing happens
until an acceptance delay time has elapsed, then the character associated with the key
is generated. If the user continues to hold down the key, again nothing happens for a
period equal to the auto-repeat delay time, and if the key is not released within that time
then multiple copies of the character will be generated and this will continue until the
user releases the key.

A keyboard can be matched to the manual abilities of different users if there is a
facility to adjust the settings of the acceptance delay time and the auto-repeat delay
time. Some users with impaired manual dexterity or hand tremors may have a tendency

to touch keys accidentally. By increasing the acceptance delay time only keys which have been touched deliberately, and held, will be registered. Other people can have the problem that having located and pressed a key they cannot remove their finger quickly. Of course, should they not remove their hand within the auto-repeat delay time they will get unwanted multiple copies of the character. There should therefore be a facility to extend the auto-repeat delay time, or to disable the auto-repeat facility entirely.

A simple, mechanical solution to the problem of accidentally touching keys in the vicinity of the target one, which may be used in conjunction or as an alternative to the adjustment of the acceptance delay time, is the addition of a *keyguard*. A keyguard is a cover for the keyboard with holes corresponding to the key positions, which provides a barrier between adjacent keys.

Another dexterity problem arises from the fact that users are often expected not to press one key at a time, but multiple chords. Restarting one popular system requires the user to press no less than three keys (CTRL, ALT and DEL) simultaneously (see **modifier key** in the glossary). This may be difficult for many users even with quite good dexterity, and quite impossible for someone using a single stick to press keys. This is not a feature of the keyboard as such, but of the **software** driven from the keyboard. Designers of the software must be aware of this difficulty and should provide a means of generating a command equivalent to a chord which can be accessed one key at a time, such as a mechanism whereby each of the keys can be pressed singly in turn (CTRL followed by ALT and then DEL, for instance) to be registered as if they had been pressed simultaneously.

Most computer keyboards resemble their counterparts on typewriters, in consisting of mechanical keys which require a certain degree of force to press and which travel a measurable distance. However, other forms of keyboard are becoming widespread, particularly *membrane* keyboards. These require minimal pressure to register a key-press. They are easier for many physically disabled people to use, but can cause other problems. A membrane keyboard can be entirely flat. This means that the keys can be located only visually and it can also make it too easy to press adjacent keys. Again, the provision of a keyguard can help to overcome these limitations. All keyboards should provide tactile cues to assist in the location of keys. In particular some form of tactile marking should be provided so that the user can find the 'home' keys without having to look. This is an aid to all users, but particularly those with a visual disability.

Human–Computer Interaction and Adaptation of the Interface

The development of the discipline of human–computer interaction has led to the design of computers which are easier to use – at least for the majority of the population. Unfortunately that effort has not been matched by similar developments in making interfaces more usable by people who differ from the average. The progress which has been made in this area has been thanks to the efforts of individuals working largely in isolation with minimal support. The common story is of a technologist, having met a disabled person, recognizing that it might be possible to apply his or her expertise to assist the person. The technologist then spends spare time, energy and inspiration developing technology for that individual.

These developers are motivated by the desire to help the individual concerned. One consequence is that they do not seek any form of publicity – even in academic journals.

Hence they do not learn of the developments of other people working in similar circumstances – and often may be 'reinventing the wheel'. Rarely are these inventions built in numbers greater than one or two, though occasionally they do lead to commercial products.

However, the economically viable manufacture of such products can be difficult because the potential market is relatively small. This is one of the reasons that developments proceed on a small scale, without commercial support. However, there is reason to believe that this is an argument which is less valid than usually assumed. Recent surveys in both the UK and the USA have revealed that there are significantly greater numbers of people with disabilities in the populations than had previously been assumed. At the same time the potential market could be increased if more international co-operation made products available in more than one country. Research initiatives by the European Community do offer good prospects in this direction.

There is another argument to support the proposition that more resources should be expended on research into developing human–machine interfaces for people with disabilities. That is that the challenge of such problems acts as a forcing function; it makes developers face up to difficult questions. Ultimately the results of such research will be of benefit to the population at large, as well as the original target group. The adaptation of computers for blind users is a good example. Conventional interfaces are overwhelmingly visual. To make an equivalent interface which is accessible to a blind person by using sounds, the interface designer will have to apply a considerable degree of novelty and inspiration. That will benefit blind people – but not only them, because the results of the research on how sounds can be used can be applied back into mainstream human–computer interaction research. The possible role of sounds in the human–computer interface is further discussed in Chapter 5.

Summary

This chapter has set the subject matter of this book in the context of the field of human–computer interaction. There are two main messages which should be drawn from this discussion. One is that the field of human–computer interaction has always been concerned with matching the interface to a range of different users, and yet up to now it has tended to ignore variations in the needs and abilities of some users which are so significant that they have a special name: disabilities. Development of interfaces for people who have disabilities is a legitimate sub-field of human–computer interaction and should be seen as such. The second point looks at the same situation in the opposite direction. If more effort is put into finding solutions for exceptional users, novel forms of interaction will be developed which will also be of use to average users.

Further Reading

The operation of stenotype keyboards is described in Downton, Newell and Arnott (1980) and their possible use in communication aids is described in Arnott and Newell (1984) and Arnott (1987).

Alm, Arnott and Newell (1989) provide a more complete description of Chat.

Betts *et al.* (1987) is the introductory paper in a special edition of the journal *Computer Graphics*, dedicated to the topic of user interface management systems (UIMSs).

Fairhurst, Bonaventura and Stephanidis (1987) discuss human–computer interaction as applied to the provision of a communication aid.

Baecker and Buxton (1987) is a collection of papers which essentially summarizes the state of the art in human–computer interaction.

Bowe (1987) reviews some of the issues surrounding the development of human–computer interfaces for disabled people.

Card, Moran, and Newell (1983) illustrate some of the ways in which psychology has been applied to the study of human–computer interaction.

Scadden and Vanderheiden (1988) represents industry's response to the adoption of section 508 of the Rehabilitation Amendments Act. It contains detailed suggestions as to how specific interface barriers can be overcome, including how keyboards can be adapted.

4 Case Studies

This chapter describes five products designed for use by disabled people which use synthetic speech. They are two communication devices, two screen readers and a reading machine. All of them have in common that they are commercially available products (see Appendix A for suppliers). Although other exciting devices are being developed, they are still in the laboratories and may never emerge as viable products. Some of these are mentioned in other parts of the book.

Communicators

Most of the requirements of a communication aid have already been discussed, under the headings of the human–machine interface and speech production. The devices studied differ mainly in the approach applied to the human–machine interface; one is textually based while the other employs a symbolic language. There are also a number of similarities, notably the level of flexibility which users are given to programme the device to match their own requirements. Between them they illustrate most of the features and techniques which were described earlier.

The second case study, Minspeak, does not in fact relate to one particular device. Minspeak is a language technique which is available on two machines, the Touch Talker™ and the Light Talker™. Although the principles are the same across the two machines, the physical interface is different.

Equalizer

Chapter 3 examined ways in which input rates can be increased. The Equalizer communicator is a significant example in that it can be operated with a single switch and incorporates nearly all of the strategies mentioned for accelerating input. The Equalizer's features include:

- word-based input;
- the facility for the user to expand the vocabulary;

- the availability of commonly used (and user-definable) phrases;
- automatic, dynamic word anticipation.

Normally input is word-based, but the user can input, letter by letter, words unknown to the system and has the option of the system remembering new words thus entered. In this way the machine adapts to the user's vocabulary. The system also learns about the language the user employs so that it can anticipate the next word in a sentence. As well as being used as a synthetic speech communicator, the Equalizer can be used as input to a **word processor**. This means that the user can not only prepare written work to be printed out, but also write speeches which will be spoken back at a later time through the synthesizer.

Input is based upon menus which are displayed on a computer screen. Items are selected in two stages through a scanning mechanism. Lines in a menu are highlighted one by one, and when the line containing the appropriate item is highlighted, the user presses the switch. That causes each item in that line to be highlighted in turn, and the item is selected by pressing the switch when it is highlighted.

Figure 4.1 shows the main menu. The lower half of the menu consists of the thirty-six most commonly used words (based on studies of general English usage), known as

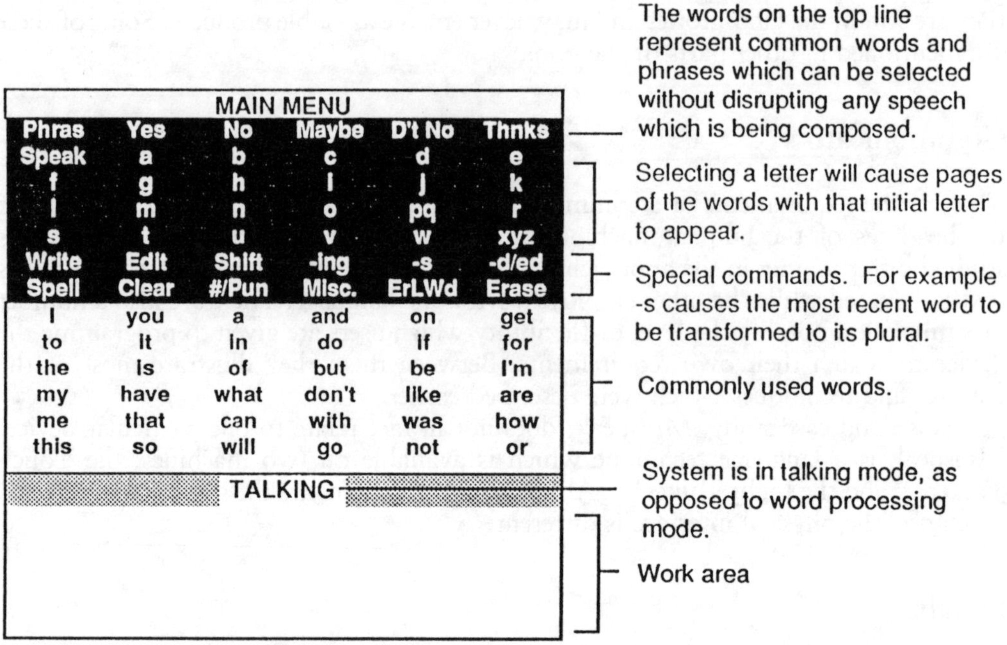

The words on the top line represent common words and phrases which can be selected without disrupting any speech which is being composed.

MAIN MENU					
Phras	**Yes**	**No**	**Maybe**	**D't No**	**Thnks**
Speak	a	b	c	d	e
f	g	h	i	j	k
l	m	n	o	pq	r
s	t	u	v	w	xyz
Write	**Edit**	**Shift**	**-ing**	**-s**	**-d/ed**
Spell	**Clear**	**#/Pun**	**Misc.**	**ErLWd**	**Erase**
I	you	a	and	on	get
to	it	in	do	if	for
the	is	of	but	be	I'm
my	have	what	don't	like	are
me	that	can	with	was	how
this	so	will	go	not	or
TALKING					

Selecting a letter will cause pages of the words with that initial letter to appear.

Special commands. For example -s causes the most recent word to be transformed to its plural.

Commonly used words.

System is in talking mode, as opposed to word processing mode.

Work area

The screen, showing the main menu. The highlighting (i.e. black background) alternates between the two topmost areas. By pressing the switch the user selects the currently highlighted area.

Figure 4.1   The main menu of the Equalizer. First, the two halves of the menu are highlighted in turn and the user must select the half containing the target.

the Quikwords. They are arranged according to frequency of use, so that the most commonly used words are in the top left-hand corner of the menu, where they can be selected most quickly. If users wish to say a word not in the Quikwords list, they must select it from an alphabetical list. These lists are accessed via the letters in the top half of the main menu. The other entries in the top half have special functions, which will be explained below.

The best way to describe the Equalizer is through an example. Word selection is based on making selections from menus. Sections of the menus are highlighted in turn by being displayed in inverse colour (i.e. white on black). Pressing the switch causes selection of the currently highlighted section. The user 'homes in' on the target word by making selections from successively smaller sections. The speed at which the highlighting moves can be programmed to suit the user's skill and dexterity.

Suppose the user wants to say: 'Tomorrow afternoon I'm going home.' First, the user

MAIN MENU					
Phras	Yes	No	Maybe	D't No	Thnks
Speak	a	b	c	d	e
f	g	h	i	j	k
l	m	n	o	pq	r
s	t	u	v	w	xyz
Write	Edit	Shift	-ing	-s	-d/ed
Spell	Clear	#/Pun	Misc.	ErLWd	Erase
I	you	a	and	on	get
to	it	in	do	if	for
the	is	of	but	be	I'm
my	have	what	don't	like	are
me	that	can	with	was	how
this	so	will	go	not	or
TALKING					

Figure 4.2   Line selection in the Equalizer. Having selected the top half of the screen, each line in that half is scanned, and the user selects the line containing the target letter, T.

selects the top half of the screen by pressing the switch when the top half of the screen is highlighted in black, as it is in Figure 4.1. That causes each line in that half of the screen to be highlighted in turn. Since the first word of the intended utterance begins with the letter T the user must select the line containing that letter, as shown in Figure 4.2.

Now each column in that line is highlighted in turn, and hence the user can select the T, as illustrated in Figure 4.3. This causes the main menu to be replaced by a menu of words – all beginning with the letter T, and arranged in alphabetical order, as shown

MAIN MENU					
Phras	Yes	No	Maybe	D't No	Thnks
Speak	a	b	c	d	e
f	g	h	i	j	k
l	m	n	o	pq	r
s	▮t▮	u	v	w	xyz
Write	Edit	Shift	-ing	-s	-d/ed
Spell	Clear	#/Pun	Misc.	ErLWd	Erase
I	you	a	and	on	get
to	it	in	do	if	for
the	is	of	but	be	I'm
my	have	what	don't	like	are
me	that	can	with	was	how
this	so	will	go	not	or
TALKING					

Figure 4.3   *Letter selection. Each letter in the selected row is now highlighted in turn, and the user presses the switch to select the T.*

Next page of words			
table	tea	tequila	thick
tablet	teach	than	thin
tabular	teacher	thank	thing
tabulate	technical	that	think
tact	technique	their	those
tactile	technician	them	thought
tailor	telescope	then	through
take	tell	theorem	throw
taken	tenacious	theory	thunder
talk	tender	therapy	tick
tan	tense	there	ticket
tangle	tent	these	tide
tap	tentative	thesis	tie
tape	tenure	they	tight
TALKING			

Figure 4.4   *Word selection, first page. The screen now switches to a menu containing words beginning with T. The user can select either the top line (which leads to another menu of words beginning with T) or one of the halves of the menu.*

tin	too	trail	trite
tint	tooth	train	trouble
tip	top	transfer	trousers
tissue	total	transform	truck
title	touch	translate	true
to be	tough	transport	trumpet
to go to	tourist	trap	trust
today	tow	travel	try
together	towel	traveller	tune
toggle	town	tree	tunnel
toilet	trace	trend	turbo
tomato	track	triangle	turn
tomorrow	trade	trim	tutor
tone	traffic	trip	type

TALKING

Figure 4.5   Word selection, second page. The user has moved to the next page of words and selected the appropriate half of the screen, line and now word.

MAIN MENU					
Phras	Yes	No	Maybe	D't No	Thnks
Speak	a	b	c	d	e
f	g	h	i	j	k
l	m	n	o	pq	r
s	t	u	v	w	xyz
Write	Edit	Shift	-ing	-s	-d/ed
Spell	Clear	#/Pun	Misc.	ErLWd	Erase
afternoon	night	morning	we	will	might
I	you	a	and	on	get
to	it	in	do	if	for
the	is	of	but	be	I'm
my	have	what	don't	like	are
me	that	can	with	was	how
this	so	will	go	not	or

TALKING

Tomorrow

Figure 4.6   The first word has been selected. The Equalizer returns to the main menu, showing the selected word in the working area. Notice that since it starts a sentence it has automatically been capitalized. The Equalizer has also made a selection of the likely next word.

in Figure 4.4. 'Tomorrow' does not appear on the displayed page, so the user must select 'Next page of words'. This will bring up another page of words beginning with T. Figure 4.5 shows that page at the point at which the user has gone through the stages of selecting the bottom half, then the line containing the target word, and then the word itself. A word has now been selected, and it has taken a total of seven switch presses.

The system now automatically returns to the main menu. The selected word is displayed in the work area, as in Figure 4.6. Notice that the initial letter has automatically been capitalized, as it is the start of a sentence. Notice also that there is a new line of words in the menu (starting with 'afternoon'). These are predictions made by Equalizer as to the next likely word. In this case, the required word, 'afternoon', is in that list, and so can be selected in three switch presses. The word will be added to the working area.

The next word is 'I'm', which is one of the Quikwords, and hence can be selected in three switch presses. Predictions are made again as to the next word, and, as shown in Figure 4.7, the required word, 'going', is among them, and so can be selected in the usual manner. Having selected 'going' another set of predictions appears, but 'home' is not among them, so the user must go through the same sort of process of selecting an individual word, as was required for 'tomorrow'.

The sentence is now complete, and to have it spoken the user just selects the word 'Speak' from the main menu. That took a total of twenty-one switch presses. The time taken to compose that utterance depends very much on the dexterity of the user. The scanning rate will be adjusted to suit the individual, to minimize the scanning time. However, suppose the user can average as little as 0.5 seconds per press, the above

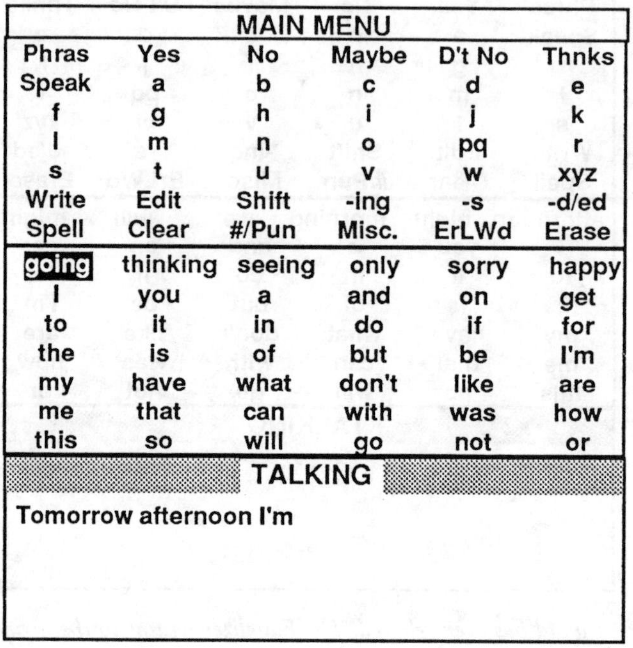

MAIN MENU					
Phras	Yes	No	Maybe	D't No	Thnks
Speak	a	b	c	d	e
f	g	h	i	j	k
l	m	n	o	pq	r
s	t	u	v	w	xyz
Write	Edit	Shift	-ing	-s	-d/ed
Spell	Clear	#/Pun	Misc.	ErLWd	Erase
going	thinking	seeing	only	sorry	happy
I	you	a	and	on	get
to	it	in	do	if	for
the	is	of	but	be	I'm
my	have	what	don't	like	are
me	that	can	with	was	how
this	so	will	go	not	or
TALKING					
Tomorrow afternoon I'm					

Figure 4.7   Selecting one of the Quikwords.

utterance would take 10.5 seconds, compared to about 1.5 seconds to speak it at normal conversational rate.

Equalizer is based upon an IBM PC-compatible computer. It is available in various configurations. It can be run from batteries, but is too large and heavy to be said to be portable – except if mounted on a wheelchair. Different synthesizers can be used, including Dectalk, the Speech Plus Calltext and the Prose 2020. Of course, such powerful **hardware** is also expensive.

An important feature of the Equalizer is that the user can operate it without assistance. As has been discussed earlier, almost by definition independence is aspired to by people with disabilities. It must be especially frustrating to have a device, such as a communicator, which increases one's independence, but which is fitted with an on–off switch which one physically cannot operate. In other words, someone else has the power to prevent you from 'talking'. This is *not* true of the Equalizer, on which the user can also control the settings of the speech volume and the scanning rate.

Clearly an Equalizer user must be literate. It can and has been used as a part of teaching basic literacy to children who lack the dexterity to use pens or pencils. Before the advent of this kind of technology such teaching was difficult, and it may not be suitable for people who have had that kind of education. Obviously it is likely to be suitable for people who have become disabled after they had acquired literacy skills. Given that it offers an unlimited vocabulary and incorporates almost every known technique to accelerate input, it is probably the best system available for those who can use it. It is difficult to see how its input rate can be improved – yet this must be achieved if conversational rates of speech are to be attained.

Equalizer is manufactured by Words+ in the United States and distributed in the UK by Cambridge Adaptive Communications. Systems tend to be built for individuals. The **software** is the important feature, which runs on standard hardware. That means the hardware can be selected and adapted for the individual. For instance, one user may require a portable, battery-powered system, while another may prefer a desk-top model. The software automatically adapts itself to individuals. Statistics as to frequency of use are maintained by the program all the time and these are also used to optimize the word prediction. If the user has to spell in a new word, he or she has the option to add it to the word list (to appear automatically in the appropriate menu). If there is insufficient **memory** for the addition the program will automatically discard the least-used word in its memory.

The Equalizer is the communicator used by Professor Stephen Hawking, probably the most celebrated user of such a device. Professor Hawking is considered by many to be the greatest physicist since Einstein, but he has motor neurone disease which led to his having a total laryngectomy. He has been able to continue to work as an academic, writing, teaching and presenting his work thanks to his use of an Equalizer. As well as numerous academic awards and prizes, he has the unusual distinction of having had a book on physics in the best-seller list for over a year (Hawking, 1988). That book was written on his Equalizer.

Minspeak, Light Talker and Touch Talker

Touch Talker and Light Talker both use the Minspeak 'language', which is described

Plate 1   Touch Talker.

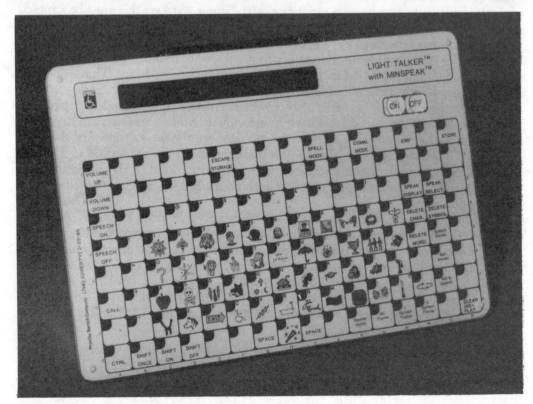

Plate 2   Light Talker.

in detail below. Minspeak is a symbolic language, in which small pictures, or icons, are associated with spoken utterances. Both devices are based on arrays of 128 cells which are effectively the keys used to make selections (see Plates 1 and 2). The icons are printed on plastic overlays which are attached over the cells. Touch Talker and Light Talker differ in the mechanics of making cell selections: Touch Talker requires the user physically to touch the cells, while Light Talker can be operated through one or two switches or a pointer. Both devices are programmable, in a manner which will be described later in this section. In this description it will be convenient to refer to the programmer and the user of the device, but these need not necessarily be different people. Everything the programmer does is through the same interface, so that there is no physical reason why the user should not programme it. At the same time someone else may do the programming for a person who lacks the necessary skills but who is quite able to use it as a communicator.

Since Touch Talker works by direct selection, it is generally quicker for those people who have sufficient manual dexterity, though it can be adapted to suit different levels of manual skill. The simplest adaptation is to attach a keyguard to help prevent the user touching the cells surrounding the target one. If that is still not sufficient protection for an individual who can touch only larger targets, overlays are available which use groups of cells to represent one symbol. For example, as shown in Figure 4.8, the eight-position overlay effectively divides the 128 cells into groups of sixteen. Touching anywhere within a group will have the effect of selecting the one symbol it represents. It is similarly easy for the programmer to configure the device to work in an eight- or thirty-two-position mode.

Light Talker differs in appearance from Touch Talker, each cell having a small red light in it. It offers a form of direct selection by way of a light pointer. This would normally be mounted on the user's head (or some other part of the body over which he or she has sufficient control). When the pointer is aimed at a cell, that cell's light illuminates, highlighting it. In this way the user can point at any given cell on the device. The action of selecting a given cell can be achieved in one of two ways: either by leaving the pointer trained on the cell for longer than a given (and programmable) interval, or by pressing a switch while the cell is highlighted.

Users who cannot employ either of the above methods can use a one- or two-switch

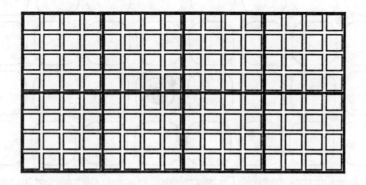

Figure 4.8 The eight-position overlay, showing how the 128 cells of Touch Talker can be divided into eight large cells.

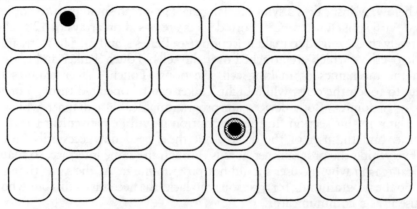

A: *The current cell is marked by a light in its corner, and the current target is the cell marked with a roundel. The user presses one switch to make the selection move down its column.*

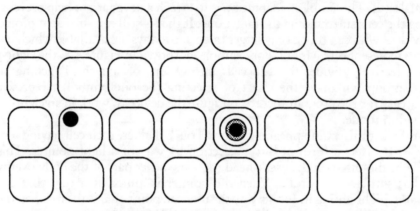

B: *Row selection. The highlight has now moved down the target row. The user would now release one switch to make the vertical movement stop, and start pressing the other switch, making it move to the right.*

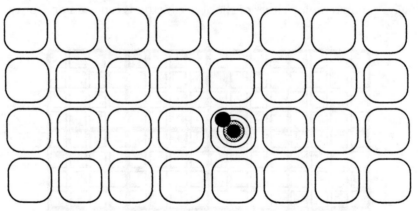

C: *Selecting the target cell. The user releases the second switch when the target is reached, so selecting it.*

Figure 4.9   *Two-switch selection on Light Talker layout*

input instead. Again the cell selection is shown through the illumination of the lights. If two switches are used, one will control the vertical selection and the other the horizontal. This is illustrated in Figure 4.9, in which the cell to be selected is marked by a 'target' icon. At any time one cell is highlighted, so that in Figure 4.9A the currently highlighted cell is marked by a black dot. By pressing one switch the user makes the highlighting move down the current column (wrapping around back to the top if the bottom row is reached). Once a cell in the correct row is highlighted (as in Figure 4.9B) the user will release the first switch, making the scanning stop. Pressing the second switch will cause the highlighting to move horizontally such that when the the target cell is highlighted the user releases the switch and that cell can be selected, as in Figure 4.9C. Again, the user can select the cell now highlighted either by pressing another switch or by simply leaving it highlighted for longer than a specified interval.

A user without the dexterity to operate two switches can use a single-switch input. Again the lights are used to highlight cells. First, a complete row of cells will be highlighted, as in Figure 4.10A. The highlighting scans down the array (at a speed which can be adjusted to suit individuals), and the user will press the switch when the row containing the target is highlighted (Figure 4.10B). Each cell in that row will then be highlighted in turn (Figure 4.10C) scanning from left to right, and the user will press the switch when the target cell is highlighted (identical to Figure 4.9C) which will be immediately selected.

This row–column scanning is a slow input technique. Increasing the scanning speed will reduce the delays, but the extent to which this will be effective depends on the user's skills and reactions, and to increase it too much will lead to an increase in the rate of errors which the user is likely to make. Errors can be very time-consuming. For instance, if the user accidentally selects the wrong row he or she must let that row be scanned three times before the machine recognizes that no selection will be made from that row and resets back to the start of the scanning operation (as in Figure 4.10A).

Light Talker can be used with eight- and thirty-two-position overlays, just as Touch Talker can. Again, facilities are available so that it can be programmed to work in this manner with a variety of scanning techniques.

Minspeak aims to minimize the number of selections required to build up an utterance. The basis of Minspeak is that by selecting sequences of icons, pre-stored utterances can be retrieved and spoken. At the simplest level of use, any utterance can be stored 'under' any cell in the array, such that if the user selects that cell the corresponding utterance will be spoken (and also displayed on a small screen).

For example, the sentence 'I would like an apple' might be stored 'under' a cell labelled with a picture of an apple, as in Figure 4.11. The essence of Minspeak is that the icon should remind the user of the corresponding message. In this case the association is obvious, but as we shall see it can become more complicated. Of course, users who program the device themselves can assign icons that they can remember according to their personal mental quirks. This is one reason why programming is made as accessible as possible. For instance, a user who is a computer enthusiast might be more aware of the Apple computer manufacturer than the fruit, and therefore use the icon in Figure 4.11 to recall the word 'computer'.

There is no reason why the utterance stored should be a whole sentence. Greater flexibility is attained by storing common building blocks, which can be combined to make sentences. As an example, instead of dedicating one cell to the sentence 'I would

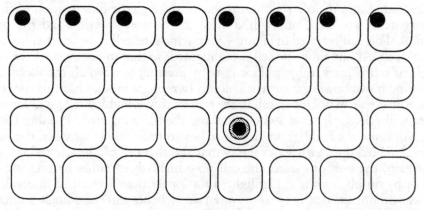

A: A complete row of cells is highlighted and the highlighting scans down the board.

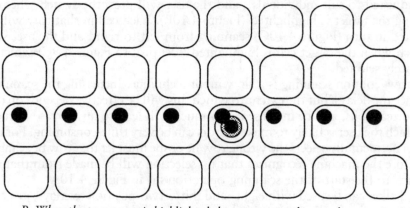

B: When the target row is highlighted the user presses the switch.

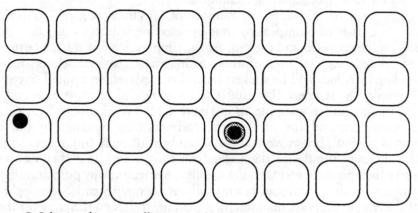

C: Selecting the target cell. Having selected the appropriate row, the left-most cell in that row is highlighted, and the highlighting then moves to the right along that row. The user will press the switch again when the target cell is reached.

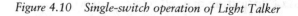

Figure 4.10   Single-switch operation of Light Talker

Figure 4.11   An apple icon, which might be used on a Minspeak overlay.

like an apple', as above, two cells might be used, one to store 'I would like' and the second with 'an apple'. That does imply that it now takes two selections to say that sentence, but it does also mean that if there is a cell containing the phrase 'to eat', the user has the possibility of saying any of the following sentences (each taking no more that three selections):

1. 'I would like an apple.'
2. 'I would like to eat.'
3. 'I would like to eat an apple.'
4. 'To eat an apple.'
5. 'An apple.'

The last two may appear a little odd, not being complete sentences, but natural conversation often consists of incomplete sentences. Consider the following dialogue:

'What would you like to eat?'
'An apple.'

Few people in normal conversation would respond, 'I would like to eat an apple.'

Given 128 cells, storing one utterance under each one would lead to a rather small, restricted vocabulary. Even someone with a minimal interest in food might have ten favourite dishes to talk about, but ten cells represent a significant proportion of 128. However, a much greater number of utterances can be accessed if the user uses sequences of icons to represent them. It is important that the sequences are constructed in such a way that they are as easy as possible to remember. One way of doing this is to build sequences systematically. For instance, rather than using the apple icon to represent 'an apple' alone, it might be used as a prefix to any food item. The two selections APPLE + CIRCLE (Figure 4.12) might elicit 'biscuit', APPLE + BATH might be 'bun', and so on. 'An apple' might now be represented as APPLE + APPLE.

In fact, any number of symbols can be combined in this way, so that some utterances might require even three or four icon selections. Once users reach such levels of complexity it is vital that they should make maximum use of the power of the icons to help them to remember how to access utterances. In other words, the icons are very much overloaded with semantic cues (which is the essential way in which this form of icons differs from their use in computer interfaces). So, different features of an icon may be significant in different contexts. The example above uses the edibility of the apple to

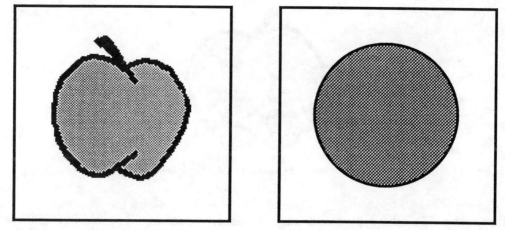

Figure 4.12   A two-symbol Minspeak command. The apple signifies food. The circle suggests a circular item of food: a biscuit.

trigger the association with food. However, in another context its initial letter might be used to make an association with another word beginning with an A. In yet another context its colour might be used, so that, for instance, if the apple icon is coloured red, APPLE + LORRY might mean 'fire engine'.

Building and using systematic combinations of symbols is facilitated by a *theme* mechanism. For instance, all utterances likely to be used in the context of a shopping expedition might be stored under a combination starting with one icon (a money icon, perhaps). On arrival at the shops the user can switch into the appropriate mode by establishing a *one-symbol* theme such that all icon selections will be automatically preceded by the appropriate symbol. The sentence 'I want to buy some food.' might be stored as MONEY + APPLE, but if the user sets up the one-symbol theme of the money icon, then only the apple icon need be selected. This will automatically be preceded by the money symbol, and so elicit the above sentence. Of course, if users really want to say the utterance stored under the apple icon alone they must escape from the shopping theme, but facilities are provided for doing this. Naturally, whenever the user wants he or she can cancel the theme – and presumably would do, in this example, once having left the shops. If themes grow more complex and specific, the user can establish two-symbol themes. Once in a two-symbol theme mode, all selections are automatically preceded by a two-symbol combination.

To a large degree the power of Minspeak arises from its programmability, because it allows each user to build it just as he or she finds it easiest to use. Programming is not difficult, but would be daunting for most new users. Hence Touch Talker and Light Talker come with pre-programmed standard overlays, which the user can use at least to start on. Programming is done by putting the device into a programming mode – for which a special 'Fixed' overlay is provided. The Fixed overlay is built in and cannot be altered. It includes a number of cells corresponding to commands as well as a set which can be used to input letters.

Adding a new utterance is quite a simple operation. The programmer presses a cell which signifies that he or she wishes to store a new utterance. The cell or cells which will represent the utterance are pressed followed by the utterance, typed letter by letter. Should the speech synthesizer not pronounce any part of the utterance very well, the programmer does have the option of entering it phonetically, but in such a way that the correct English spelling will still be displayed on the screen. Having stored this new utterance, whenever the user presses the associated cell or cells it will be spoken, and displayed on the screen.

As has been hinted at above, cells can be used for control as well as to store utterances. For example, one cell (or combination of cells) can be used to issue the command to establish a one-symbol theme. In fact, quite a large number of functions are accessed by selecting cells, such as having the contents of the display spoken, control of the volume and pitch of the speech and suchlike. It is up to the programmer which of these functions users can have access to, and which cells they must select to evoke them. The Fixed has cells corresponding to all of the functions available, and the programmer can add functions to his or her own custom overlay essentially by copying them from the Fixed overlay to the custom overlay, specifying which cells must be selected from the custom overlay to evoke each function.

Standard overlays allow the user to access the device without a lot of effort to learn to program it. An extension of the standard overlay is the Minspeak Application Program or MAP. MAPs are carefully designed overlays which have been optimized to suit the requirements of particular groups of users. These have been developed by experienced Minspeak programmers who have been able to put a great deal of thought (and experiments) into making easily remembered associations between symbols and utterances. Of course, users have to learn those associations, rather than building their own, although they can always modify the program.

At the time of writing four MAPs are commercially available: Words Strategy, which is designed for users aged fourteen and upwards; Language, Learning and Living, which is intended for adolescents with learning difficulties; Interaction, Education and Play for three- to twelve-year-olds; and Power Play, which should be accessible to children as young as two, and up to five. It can be expected that more MAPs will become available in time.

As an example, the sentence, 'Tomorrow afternoon I'm going home.' would be constructed as follows if the Language, Learning and Living (LLL) MAP were in use. The example demonstrates the sorts of explanations which can be employed to help the user remember the use of the icons. It also well illustrates the way icons are heavily overloaded, performing different roles in different contexts. Users (who would probably have learning difficulties) would not be given the complex explanations outlined below, when being taught to use LLL.

Refer to Figure 4.13 for pictures of the icons involved. 'Tomorrow' is accessed by the two icons WATCH + RING. The watch is associated with different time concepts. For instance, 'today' is accessed by selecting WATCH twice. Thinking of 'two-day' helps the user remember this. 'Yesterday' is WATCH plus the icon which comes before it (i.e. to the left of it). Hence, 'tomorrow' is WATCH plus the icon which comes after it, which happens to show a ring. An alternative explanation would be to point out how many rings the word 'tOmOrrOw' contains.

'Afternoon' is another temporal concept, so it also involves the watch. WATCH + SUNRISE is 'morning'. An icon with a sun on it follows the SUNRISE icon, and afternoon follows morning, so 'afternoon' is WATCH + SUN. Again there is an alternative

Figure 4.13   *The icons from the Language, Learning and Living Minspeak Application Program, which would be used in constructing the utterance, 'Tomorrow afternoon I'm going home.'*

explanation, based on the fact that noon is when the sun is at its highest.

The pronoun I is generated by the EYE icon and the verb 'to be' is based on the BEE icon, so that 'I'm' is EYE + BEE. The verb 'to go' is based on the CAR icon – you can go places in a car. To generate 'going' you have to signal the part of the verb (present participle), and that is done with the SWING icon. This might be explained as 'swing' rhymes with '-ing', or 'the girl is swing*ing*'. Hence, 'going' is SWING + CAR. All buildings are associated with the HOUSE icon. Most people expect to find their mother at home, hence 'home' is HOUSE + MOTHER.

So, the sample sentence can be generated in just ten selections using the LLL MAP in Minspeak. The number of switch presses would depend on whether Touch Talker or Light Talker is used. For Touch Talker this would be just ten presses (of the cells directly). For Light Talker it takes two switch presses to select any one icon (for either two-switch or single-switch selection), so twenty presses would be required. The time to make the selection would depend on the dexterity of the user and the scanning rate selected. A skilled two-switch user should be quicker than a single-switch user.

Although the physical selection techniques of Minspeak and the Equalizer bear some resemblance, there is clearly a great difference in their input techniques and it is this which would probably be the major consideration in selecting between the two. One obvious advantage of Minspeak is that the user need not be literate. Even someone with minimal language skills should be able to use a suitably programmed machine, and use it to develop skills. The flexibility of Minspeak means that it is entirely up to the user (or the programmer) what the size of the speech building blocks will be, and this is something which is likely to be altered as the user learns and develops. For instance a child with minimal language skills might have a eight-overlay with a sentence under each cell, each expressing some basic message ('Yes', 'No', 'I'm hungry', etc.).

At the other end of the scale extremely complex programs can be built up. As described, these rely on overloading the icons. Although this may seem to be unnatural and complex, it is claimed to be built on linguistic principles, and it does seem to work for a significant number of users.

Both Minspeak devices run on rechargeable batteries. The user is given plenty of warning should the level of the batteries become low. In the extreme the device will shut itself down in an attempt to conserve energy so that the contents of the memory will not be lost. The contents can be backed up on to a computer floppy disc. This is a sensible precaution to preserve the programs of customized overlays, which could be lost if memory should be lost for any reason. To make such a back-up the user will need a computer (an Acorn BBC or an Apple II), a connector and software to run on the computer.

Although their primary use is as communication aids, both Touch Talker and Light Talker can also be used as terminals to microcomputers. They are quite portable, measuring approximately 33 × 23 × 9 cm (13 × 9 × 3.5 inches) and weighing around 2.25 kg (5 lb). They can be carried, either by an integral handle or a protective carrying case, or can be mounted on a wheelchair. Two forms of on–off switch are available. The standard one would not be operable by most users, but they should be able to use the optional additional one. The older version used an Echo™ synthesizer, but the later version used the better quality of the Smoothtalker.

Light Talker and Touch Talker are manufactured by the Prentke Romich Company in the United States and distributed in the UK by Liberator Ltd. Liberator offers a comprehensive back-up service, including training, a telephone help-line and a repair/replacement service.

Screen Readers

As discussed in the previous chapter, in order to gain access to computers blind people need the output from the computer (which is predominantly visual) converted into a form which can be read through the sense of touch or hearing. As computer output is mostly in a textual form, the obvious translation into an auditory form is to use synthetic speech. Two approaches can be taken to this. One is to write **applications** which are designed to give speech output and the other is to provide a means of adapting the output of standard visual programs into synthetic speech.

The screen readers which will be discussed in this chapter are examples of the latter approach, that of adaptation. As briefly discussed earlier, and illustrated in Figure 3.2, this technique implies adapting the human–computer interface by interposing a new layer between the computer and the user. This essentially accepts the (visual) output from the computer and transforms it such that the blind user can access it (that is, in an auditory form). The disadvantage of this approach is that the computer's visual output may not lend itself to transformation into another format. The extreme example of this is the graphical user interface, which is discussed fully in Chapter 5.

Even though the adaptation approach may thus lead to interfaces which are difficult to use, it does have a number of advantages. Principally, it should be possible to produce one adaptation which will make most applications accessible to blind users (though not all of them; recall the discussion on compatibility in Chapter 2). In other words, it is not necessary to develop a talking word processor and a talking spreadsheet – with all the resources that would be required for such redundant development – two standard visual programs should be accessible through the one adaptation.

A glance at any software catalogue will demonstrate that a vast array of programs is available. There are hundreds of versions of programs which do essentially the same job, such as word processors, and yet there is room in the market for them all. Although superficially one word processor is much like any other, it is found that advocates of one or other program are likely to defend it with the sort of vehemence that is normally reserved for discussions on religion and politics. Given such variety, it is only fair that users who are blind should have access to a similar range of choices. This is possible if a means can be provided to adapt the existing visual programs.

It must always be borne in mind that the potential market for any equipment for use by blind people is very small. The raw material of software production is human thought – so it is very labour-intensive and the costs can be recouped only by high prices or large sales. It is therefore commercially unviable to produce large amounts of software which will be used only by blind people, and the market is certainly not large enough for the sort of duplication of programs found in the general market.

Standardization is very important in commercial settings. Companies will often choose standard applications which their employees must use. The major advantage of this is in the sharing of data. For instance, a word-processed document created by one person can be edited by another and passed on for printing to a third. There are also the economies of scale which come when the company purchases multiple copies of the same program. These benefits of standardization should extend to all employees, including any who are disabled. So again, it is advantageous if a blind employee can use visual software with the assistance of an adaptation. This is also important psychologically, in that the person is aware that minimal special accommodation is being made for him or her. The screen reader is an clear example of such a generalized adaptation. The general idea is that text is displayed on the computer screen, and the screen reader provides facilities to examine that screen and convert its contents into speech.

It is often difficult to draw a clear distinction between hardware and software (see the glossary) and this is well illustrated in examining different screen readers. Some take the form of a hardware addition to a standard computer, while others are embodied almost entirely as software. In fact, Telesensory's Vert screen reader is available in different versions which are based on these extreme approaches (see Appendix A). The obvious difference between the two approaches is the cost: hardware-based screen readers are much more expensive, but for the extra outlay the hardware-based device has greater power, flexibility and compatibility.

The software-based approach will be described first, and then the hardware solution can be described in the same terms. First, it is necessary to describe how a standard application displays information on the screen. The application must be loaded in the computer's memory in order to run. When it is to display some text on the screen, it copies it to a special area of the memory, known as the *screen buffer*, and the hardware ensures that the screen is automatically altered to display the new text. The screen buffer is therefore effectively a duplicate image of what is on the screen – in a form which a program can handle, so a screen reader does not 'look' at the screen as such (there is no camera attached to the screen), instead it examines the screen buffer.

The screen reader is a program which runs at the same time as the application being adapted. Any program must be held in memory to be run, and in a software-based screen reader that program must share the computer's memory with the application program (and the screen display image). A program which shares memory is this way is said to be co-resident – also sometimes known as a 'terminate and stay resident', or TSR. The operation is illustrated in Figure 4.14. The application program is loaded in memory and specifies what is to be displayed on the screen by putting it into the screen buffer.

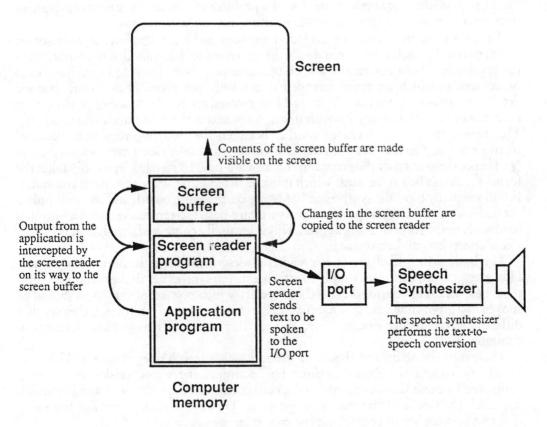

Figure 4.14   Memory allocation and interaction for a screen reader. The screen reader software resides in memory, along with the application program and the screen map. It intercepts information which the application would normally send directly to the screen so that it can send it to the speech synthesizer as necessary. It then passes the information on to the screen, unchanged.

The screen reader is loaded in a separate part of memory. It also has access to the screen buffer and can examine the contents. It then performs text-to-speech translation via a speech synthesizer. As well as passively examining what is on the screen, the screen reader can also detect changes as they happen. So, as suggested in Figure 4.14, data which are *en route* from the application to the screen are intercepted by the screen reader, which interprets them before passing them on (unchanged) to the screen buffer.

An important feature of this form of adaptation is its transparency. The application program is not modified, it works just as normal regardless of the fact that its output to the screen is being intercepted and, similarly, the screen display mechanism is unaltered.

One of the difficulties of implementing a software screen reader is that the parts of memory allocated to the different components must never overlap. The smaller the memory of the computer, the harder it is to achieve this. A screen reader with sophisticated control facilities and good text-to-speech translation can become a significantly large program and it becomes harder to find a piece of memory large enough to accommodate it, without disturbing anything else. Finding enough memory for the co-resident program becomes less of a problem all the time as memory continues to become cheaper and therefore more plentiful in standard systems.

To run a program it must be loaded in memory and must also have a **processor** on which to run. In a software screen reader the screen reader not only shares memory with the application, but the two also run on the same processor. This can be achieved even on computers which are really intended to run only one program at a time, but the details are not important here. In the hardware-based approach the screen reader has its own processor and memory (though it still must access the computer's screen buffer). This means there is no memory conflict between the two (whereby two pieces of software attempt to use the same piece of memory), and much less restriction on the size (and hence the power) of the program. A hardware-based screen reader usually takes the form of a circuit board (or card) which must be fitted into a spare slot in the computer. It will normally have the synthesizer hardware on the same board, and so needs only a connection to an external speaker. Even software-based screen readers need additional hardware, in the form of a synthesizer. This is normally connected through an I/O port (see Connections and compatibility, in Chapter 2).

The basic principle of the screen reader, as described above, is quite a simple one. However, it is not sufficient simply to attach a speech synthesizer to the computer; there must be a means to control the speech, to specify which portion of the screen should be spoken at a given time, and in what manner. It is in the control interface to the user that different screen reader designs vary, though they nearly all have some features in common.

There must be an area of the screen around which speech operations act. This may loosely be named the *speech cursor*.[1] For example, the screen reader will have a command to cause the word under the speech cursor to be spoken, and another which will elicit the whole of the line occupied by it. The case studies below illustrate very different approaches to controlling the speech cursor.

---

[1] Unfortunately the word 'cursor' is somewhat overused in computing. The speech cursor and text cursor referred to here should not be confused with the mouse pointer cursor component of graphical user interfaces.

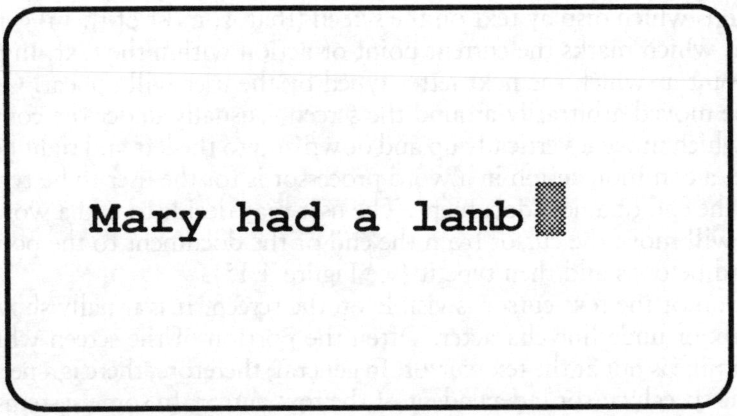

Mary had a lamb

A: *The text cursor is marked by the grey box, and is currently at the end of the text which has just been typed in.*

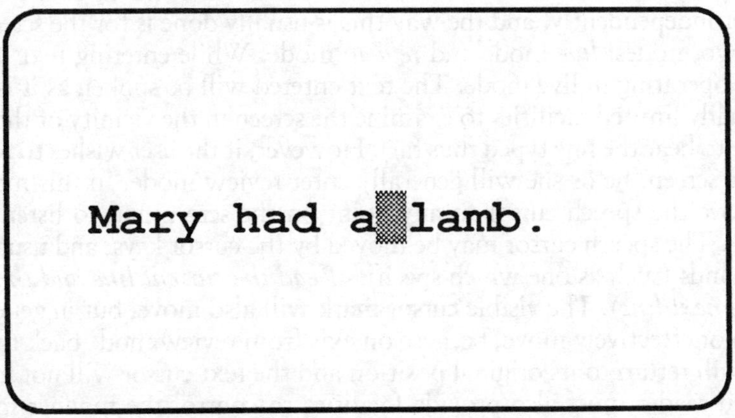

Mary had a lamb.

B: *The user now moves the cursor back (using the cursor key, ←) to the point at which a new word is to be inserted.*

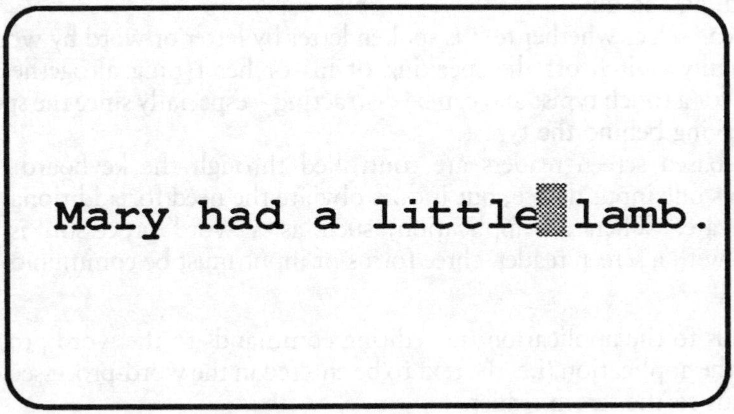

Mary had a little lamb.

C: *The user now types in the new word.*

Figure 4.15   *The text cursor*

Applications which display text on the screen (that is, most of them) generally have a text cursor, which marks the current point of action within the text. In particular it marks the point at which the next letter typed by the user will appear. Generally the cursor can be moved arbitrarily around the screen – usually under the control of four cursor keys which move it vertically up and down and to the left and right horizontally. For example, a common action in a word processor is for the user to be typing in text, adding it to the end of a new document. The user may decide to add a word in the last sentence, so will move the cursor from the end of the document to the point at which the new word belongs and then type it (see Figure 4.15).

The position of the text cursor is visible on the screen. It is usually shown as either a flashing box or underline character. Often the portion of the screen which the user wants to examine is not at the text cursor. In general, therefore, there is a need to be able to control the speech cursor independent of the text cursor. In some systems (including the Frank Audiodata, described below) the two are quite independent, whereas in others they are closely linked, to the extent that the speech cursor is always at the same point as marked by the text cursor. However, there is still a need to be able to control the speech cursor independently, and the way this is usually done is for the screen reader to operate in two modes: *live* mode and *review* mode. While entering text the user will probably be operating in live mode. The text entered will be spoken as it is typed, and there are usually limited facilities to examine the screen in the vicinity of the text cursor (for instance to hear the line typed thus far). However, if the user wishes to roam further afield on the screen, he or she will generally enter review mode. In this mode the user is free to move the speech cursor to any point on the screen and to listen to the text around there. The speech cursor may be moved by the cursor keys, and usually through other commands (such as one which specifies *Read the current line and then move the cursor to the next line*). The visible cursor mark will also move, but in general the text cursor does not effectively move, because on exit from review mode back to live mode, the marker will return to its original position and the text cursor will not have moved.

The screen reader must also provide facilities to control the manner in which the speech is produced. For instance, the user should be able to specify the speed at which it is generated, whether typing will be echoed character by character or only as each word is completed, and so on.

The user can select whether text is spoken letter by letter or word by word. Also, the user can usually switch off the speaking of his or her typing altogether; it is often unnecessary for a touch typist and can be distracting – especially since the speech is often slow and lagging behind the typist.

Software-based screen readers are controlled through the keyboard. This rather overloads this one input device, but it does obviate the need for additional (expensive) input hardware. When an application, such as a word processor, is running in conjunction with a screen reader, three forms of input must be communicated through the keyboard:

1. commands to the application (i.e. editing commands to the word processor);
2. input to the application (i.e. the text to be entered in the word-processed document);
3. commands to the screen reader.

These have to be distinguishable and this is achieved by exploiting the extended character set of the keyboard. Anything typed using single keys is by default treated as input to the application. Conventionally, command codes to an application are generated by use of the CTRL **modifier key**.

Having introduced these basic concepts, we go on to examine two very different examples of screen readers, one very much hardware-based, while the second is a popular, mainly software, system.

Dolphin Hal

As was pointed out earlier, there are two approaches to the design of screen readers. The Frank Audiodata is at one extreme, hardware-based but expensive. Hal is at the other end of the spectrum – software-based and very inexpensive. It runs on PC-compatibles and PS/2s^{TM}. The only hardware component is the speech synthesizer, the controlling program is co-resident and the user interacts only through the keyboard. Older versions of Hal used the Dolphin Mimic synthesizer, but current versions use the Dolphin Apollo, which has remarkably high quality for such a low-cost unit.

Hal does operate in two modes, as described above, referred to as *live* mode and *reading* mode. In live mode the ALT modifier key is used to pass commands to Hal. In other words any keypress which is accompanied by the ALT key is interpreted as a command by Hal. All other keypresses are passed on to the program which is running. All commands are single codes, and the designers have attempted to use letters which have some mnemonic significance, and so are easier to remember. For instance, the command ALT-L causes the current *line* to be spoken, while ALT-S adjusts the *speed* of

Command	Effect
ALT-F	Load or save a parameter file
ALT-G	Speak the current row and column numbers
ALT-I	Speak the character at the current cursor position
ALT-J	Enter reading mode
ALT-K	Speak the current line up to the cursor
ALT-L	Speak the current line
ALT-M	Silence (mute) the speech
ALT-N	Pass the next character to the system
ALT-O	Speak the word at the current cursor position
ALT-P	Speak the contents of a window
ALT-S	Set the speed of the speech
ALT-Y	Search for highlighted text and speak it

Table 4.1   Commands available when Hal is in live mode.

the speech. Of course the possibility of maintaining a mnemonic mapping is limited if one uses single letters. Hence, for instance, the command to enter reading mode is ALT-J. Some applications respond to ALT codes, and it is possible to pass these through Hal to the application if necessary, by way of an *escape* command; ALT-N passes the *next* character through. For instance, if the user needs to type ALT-L to the application he or she would type ALT-N ALT-L.

Users can select whether what they type should be spoken, and whether that should be letter by letter or word by word. Anything printed on the screen by the software is also spoken. There are limited facilities for examining the screen, as summarized in Table 4.1 (some of the entries in the table are explained further below). To examine the contents of the screen fully the user must move into reading mode (by typing ALT-J).

In reading mode the application and system are suspended and the user interacts directly with Hal, so that all keypresses are interpreted by it. Speech is controlled by single-letter and ALT commands, while CTRL codes are used to change the style of the speech. The cursor can be moved by letter commands, or by the cursor keys, in which case the movement is accompanied by speech. Notice that there is no distinction between the text and speech cursors. A much larger number of commands is available, and a selection of them is summarized in Table 4.2. Most of the ALT commands from live mode also work in reading mode.

The operation of Hal can be illustrated by a short hypothetical example. A user (who will be assumed to be female) wishes to use a word processor to insert a new paragraph in the middle of a file she created previously. She launches the word processor. As it sets up the screen it probably outputs a lot of text, so the user presses ALT-M to silence this incomprehensible and time-consuming speech. Once that has settled down and the required file has been loaded the user needs to locate the section of text she wishes to alter. Suppose she recalls that there is a particular word in the paragraph preceding the point at which she wishes to insert new text. She would use the word processor's search facility to locate the paragraph. She enters the *search* command, and types in the target word (which is spoken as she types). The word processor locates the first occurrence of the word, and moves the cursor to it. The user must now check whether this is the correct occurrence of the word, which she does by entering ALT-L. From the context she realizes that this is not the appropriate occurrence, so she makes the word processor continue searching. She checks the next occurrence in the same way, but this time she cannot be sure whether this is the right one just by hearing the line. At this point she is likely to move into reading mode, by typing ALT-J.

Typing U three times she moves the cursor back in the paragraph. As the cursor moves, Hal makes beeping noises which give the user some indication of the contents of the lines moved through. Then she listens to those three lines using the cursor down key (↓). Having established that this is the correct paragraph the user must re-enter live mode, so that she can enter the new paragraph, so she presses the ENTER key. Using ALT-L and the cursor keys the user moves the cursor to the blank line at the end of the paragraph. She can then enter the new paragraph, with each word being spoken back to her. Having entered it, she may wish to proofread it. Using reading mode as before, she can move back and listen to the paragraph. On locating a line containing a word which sounds suspiciously as if it is misspelt, she homes in on it, using CTRL-→. When she hears the suspect word spoken again, she has it spelt out letter by letter, using the → key. She finds that there is an extra letter in the word. To correct it she will need to

Command	Effect
L	Speak the line to the right of the cursor
R	Speak the current word
C	Speak the current character and move cursor right one character
M	Set a marker
G	Go to a marker
W	Set or define a window
X	Speak the column number of the cursor position
Y	Speak the line number of the cursor position
↑	Move cursor up one line and speak new line
↓	Move cursor down one line and speak new line
→	Move cursor right one character and speak new character
←	Move cursor left one character and speak new character
CTRL-→	Move cursor right one word and speak new word
CTRL-←	Move cursor left one word and speak new word
F	Find a character
T	Move cursor to top of screen
B	Move cursor to bottom of screen
U	Move cursor up a line
D	Move cursor down a line
CTRL-P	Set whether punctuation is spoken
CTRL-K	Set level of keyboard echo (off, characters or words)
ENTER	Exit reading mode

Table 4.2   Commands available when Hal is in reading mode. The single-letter commands are not generated with the ALT *key, though the commands in live mode are also available.*

enter live mode, but on exit from reading mode the cursor will not remain in its current position, but return to wherever it was when reading mode was entered. However, by entering X and Y the user can have the current position (line and column number) of the cursor spoken. She then presses ENTER and now uses the cursor keys (which now work with the word processor, but which do still cause the letters traversed to be spoken) to move the cursor back to the location of the error. She will be guided back to the same screen position by using the ALT-G command. Once at the correct position she enters ALT-R to check that the cursor is on the erroneous extra character. Pressing the DEL key will remove it. The modified and corrected file can now be written to disc and closed.

This example illustrates a number of wider points. First, it does show how complex tasks can be carried out by a blind user. However, it also shows how difficult that can be, compared with the amount of effort which would be required by a sighted user. The problems fall into three categories:

1. those which are inherent in manipulating text represented in speech;
2. those resulting from the fact that the screen reader attempts to adapt a word processor which was designed to be used in a visual manner;
3. those which are a result of the software-based approach to implementing the screen reader.

The first two are inherent in the use of screen readers, and serve to illustrate general points made earlier. The last will become more apparent when contrasted with the hardware-based Frank Audiodata, in the next section.

The complexity of correcting the spelling error is clear. The need for separate reading and live modes is a consequence of software-based implementation and the fact that the text and speech cursors are identical. To make the correction the user must return to live mode but in so doing the cursor does not stay in the same position – a result of the fact that the screen reader is an add-on adaptation which attempts to interact with the application in a way which was not anticipated by the application designer. The strategy of finding the cursor's co-ordinates has to be applied, but this is an example of the extra memory load placed on the user, who must remember the line and column number while exiting reading mode and relocating the cursor. Of course, writing a quick note of the numbers is out of the question.

Some of the complex and tedious navigation problems can be overcome by making use of marker and window facilities which Hal provides. Markers can be set at points on the screen of particular interest. For instance, an application may have a status line at a particular, fixed position. So that the user can consult it quickly she might set a marker at that point. Markers can be set in reading mode. The user locates the appropriate point on the screen and enters M, followed by any single letter (e.g. 'a'). That letter now labels the marker. Thereafter (in reading mode) the user enters GA to move the cursor to that point and can then hear the contents of the status line (by entering ALT-L).

Windows work in a similar manner, but define two-dimensional areas of the screen. For example, some programs use part of the screen to display helpful cues or menus, while the information the user is interacting with is displayed on the rest of the screen. In such a case the user might define two windows, corresponding to those separate areas. Windows are also defined in reading mode. The user moves the cursor to the point which will form the top left-hand corner of the window. She then enters WS ('window start') and then any digit from 1 to 9. The cursor is then moved to the bottom right-hand corner, and the user enters WE ('window end'). In either live or reading mode, the user can specify that the contents of a window should be spoken, by entering ALT-P, followed by the number of the required window. In reading mode the user can examine the contents of a window by entering W followed by the window number. The cursor will jump to the start of that window. It can then be examined using the usual commands, but these will operate only within that window. Thus, for instance, once the cursor has been moved to the right-hand edge of the window, it is not possible to move it any further to the right. The whole screen can be treated as a window. It is automatically referred to as window number 0.

Having defined a set of windows and markers which match a particular application the user can save the definitions in a file so that she does not have to redefine them every time she runs that application. The definition file can be reloaded at any time, via the ALT-F command.

There are a number of parameters of the speech style which the user can control. One of the most important is the speed. Others include whether punctuation should be spoken or not, whether text should be spoken word by word, character by character or not at all and whether capital letters should be declared as such (i.e. 'A' is pronounced as 'Cap A' if this option is on).

The Dolphin Hal is the most popular screen reader in the UK. This is because it provides all the functionality that users are likely to need – at a very low cost. The next section describes another screen reader, which many more users might like to use, if only they could afford it.

Frank Audiodata

The Frank Audiodata is the Rolls-Royce of screen readers, in that it is expensive, but one is paying for quality. Designers of most software-based screen readers tend to concentrate on keeping the product inexpensive. A hardware-based approach, as embodied by the Audiodata, will be more expensive but at the same time more effort can be expended on making the interface better suited to users. Whereas other screen readers are controlled through the keyboard, the Audiodata has separate controls for the screen reader alone.

The original version of the Audiodata (Audiodata 1) was released in the early 1980s. It was succeeded by Audiodata 2, a new version of the hardware, in 1988. Since then there has been a flurry of updates to the software, resulting in the Audiodata 3 version. It is available in a variety of configurations. For partially sighted users, the speech output can be supplemented by large print, while there is also the option of adding either a forty- or eighty-column soft braille display. The same mechanism is used to control the speech, braille and large print displays (see below). The options represent the valuable possibility of redundancy in the human–computer interface. In principle a suitably skilled user could see, hear and feel the text simultaneously, though in reality the intention is that a partially sighted user might use the large print backed up by speech or a blind braille reader might use braille and speech. However, this section describes only the speech-based aspects of the Audiodata.

In the Frank Audiodata, control of the speech cursor is independent of the text cursor. Speech is controlled by way of two sliders, known as *tasos* ('tactile-acoustic screen orientation') mounted around the computer keyboard. One slides vertically and controls which line of text on the screen will be spoken while the other operates similarly in the horizontal dimension, controlling the column of interest (see Figure 4.16 and Plate 3). Each has a button on the top and pressing these causes the current region to be spoken. For instance, if the button on the vertical (line) taso is pressed the current line of text will be spoken. Speech is produced only so long as the button is held down. The horizontal (column) taso enables the user to listen to part of a line.

Plate 3   Frank Audiodata.

In fact the column taso is an optional component of the Audiodata 3. It is possible to access the computer screen using only the row taso, as incorporated in the audiobox (see Plate 3). The advantage of this is that the audiobox alone is less expensive and more portable – such that it is feasible to use it with portable, lap-top computers. The disadvantage is that it does not give as powerful, two-dimensional control facilities.

Other auditory cues are given to users to guide their movement of the tasos. 'Beeps' are sounded as they move to the next line or column position. Different pitches of tones give users more information about the contents of the screen. If the line taso is moved down lines with text on them a repeated sequence of five pitches is heard. A blank line is marked by another, distinctive high-pitched tone, so that users can recognize the boundaries of paragraphs. A deep tone is used to signal that the taso is on the same line as the cursor. Similar cues are used to guide the movement of the column taso.

The Audiodata 1 was an adaptation of the IBM PC. It is significant that it was very much specific to that machine, and could not be used with even very similar computers: none of the PC-compatibles. It consisted of a circuit card and a keyboard. The circuit board has to be slotted into the computer and the keyboard replaces the standard IBM one. The tasos are located on the keyboard, along with knobs to control the volume and

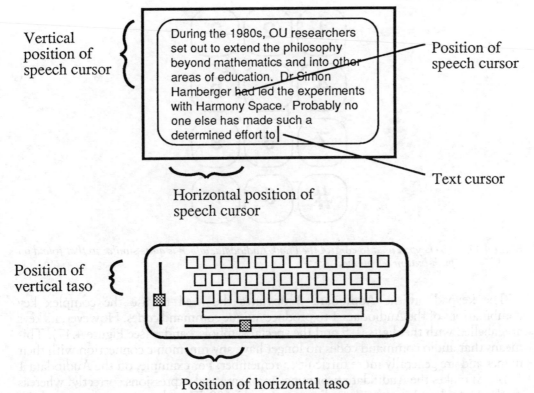

Figure 4.16 Controlling the Frank Audiodata. The speech cursor is independent of the text cursor. Its position is invisible and corresponds to the row and column of the screen as specified by the vertical and horizontal tasos, respectively.

pitch of the speech, and the speaker out of which the speech is produced. Although the family of PC-compatibles have been the most popular microcomputers, many users do not prefer those manufactured by IBM, but that choice was not available to anyone who wanted to use the Audiodata 1. Also, in the latter 1980s PCs were beginning to be phased out in favour of the PS/2 range. The Audiodata 2 and 3 were developed partly to give users access to a much wider set of computers. The Audiodata 3 can be used with most PC- and PS/2-compatibles. The standard keyboard is no longer replaced, but instead it is positioned upon a stand which contains the tasos. In addition there is a separate, twelve-button keypad through which the audio commands are entered.

The tasos control the selection of the area of the screen to be spoken, but additional control must be provided and on the Audiodata 1 this was done through commands entered on the keyboard. Commands to the Audiodata are specified by use of the ALT and **function keys**. The combination ALT+F10 (generated by holding down the ALT key and pressing F10) is called AUDIO and is followed by the user pressing one of the other keys, which is then treated as a command to the Audiodata. For example AUDIO-U switches on an option whereby upper-case letters are identified when read to the user by being preceded by a high pitched tone.

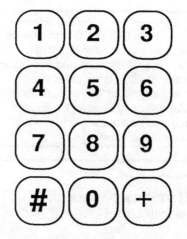

Figure 4.17   The keypad used to control the Frank Audiodata, which is quite similar to that found on push-button telephones.

The keypad on the Audiodata 3 obviates the need to use the complex key combinations of the Audiodata 1 to produce unique command codes. However, its keys are labelled with the digits 0–9 and the special symbols * and + (see Figure 4.17). This means that audio command codes no longer have any mnemonic connection with their names and are generally more difficult to remember. For example, on the Audiodata 1 AUDIO-M makes the Audiodata pronounce mathematical expressions correctly, whereas on the Audiodata 2 the corresponding command is *38. The + key operates as a modifier key, so that the user must hold it down while simultaneously pressing another key. Commands which are specified in this way are always single digits.

The differences between the Audiodata and Hal can be illustrated by pursuing the same scenario as earlier. The user launches the word processor and uses it to search for the appropriate word, as before. The text cursor will now be positioned on the word but the speech cursor will have to be moved to the same line to check the context. Having ascertained that it is not the required paragraph, the user searches again. The way most word processors work, it is quite likely that the line containing the target word will be positioned on the same screen line each time, so that the vertical taso will probably already be on the same line. To check back in the paragraph the user moves the vertical taso up three lines – which are marked by beeps as the taso moves. She then presses the vertical taso button, hears the line, moves it down one line and listens to that, and so on. Having decided that this is the correct paragraph, the user locates the blank line succeeding it by moving the vertical taso down. The blank line will be apparent because its beep will be a distinctly high-pitched one. The user presses the vertical taso button just to check.

Now the speech cursor is in the appropriate position for the new paragraph – but the text cursor is not. Entering +7 achieves the desired effect. Having got the text cursor in position, the user now enters the new paragraph.

The user then proofreads the paragraph. The position of the speech cursor relative to the paragraph will depend on how long it is. If the paragraph is a short one, the vertical taso will be still be on the blank line at its head. However, if the paragraph is so long

A

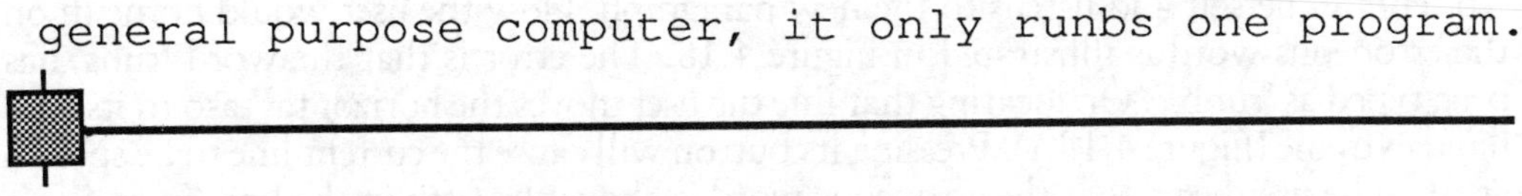

general purpose computer, it only runbs one program.

A: Having located the line containing an error, the column (horizontal) taso is moved to the left-hand edge. If the user presses the button on the column taso the current line will be read out.

B

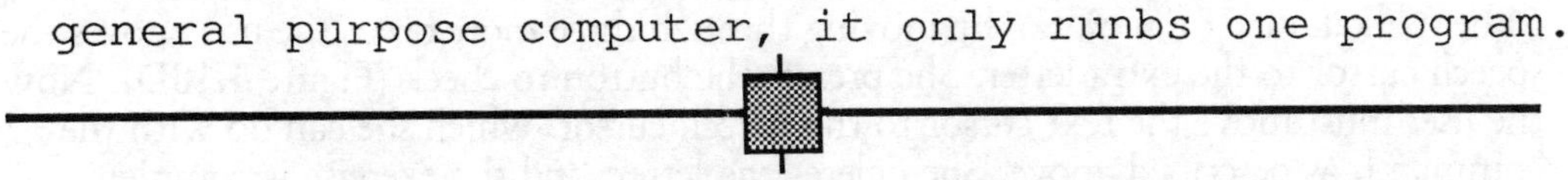

general purpose computer, it only runbs one program.

B: The user moves the taso to the right, counting the number of words traversed, as signalled by high-pitched tones marking the spaces between them. Pressing the button now causes the line to the right of the current position to be spoken.

C

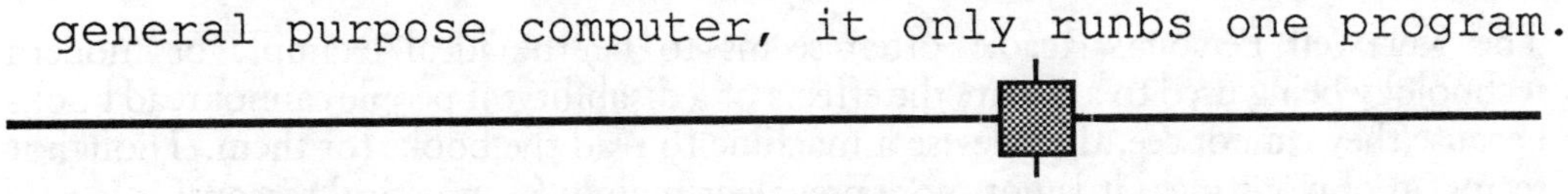

general purpose computer, it only runbs one program.

C: The user moves the taso two words further, and then one more column (beep) to the right so that it is on the first letter of the erroneous word. She checks it has been located by pressing the taso button, which will cause the word to be spelt out.

D

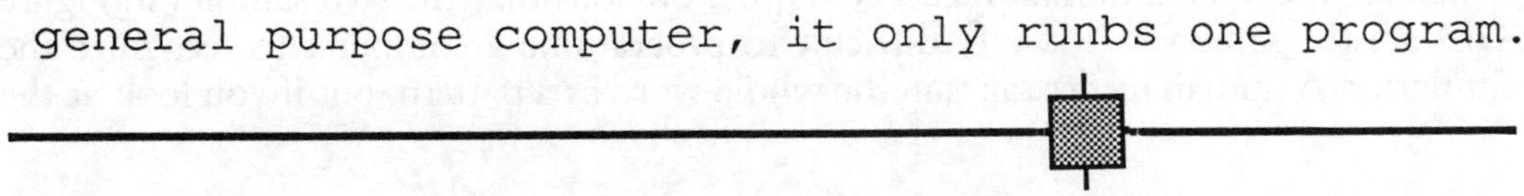

general purpose computer, it only runbs one program.

D: The user has moved the taso to the position of the extra letter.

Figure 4.18   Locating a word processing error with the Frank Audiodata, using the column taso

that it would have extended beyond the bottom of the screen, the word processor will have scrolled the text to keep the text cursor on screen. Using the vertical taso, the user reorientates herself and listens to the new paragraph. How the user would home in on the erroneous word is illustrated in Figure 4.18. The error is that the word 'runs' has been typed as 'runbs'. On locating that line the user moves the horizontal taso to its left-hand extreme (Figure 4.18A). Pressing its button will cause the current line to be spoken again. The user hears that the erroneous word is about the fifth in the line (in fact it is the sixth). The user can use beeps generated as the taso is moved to move toward it. Spaces are marked by high-pitched beeps, so she moves the taso and counts four such beeps. She then presses the taso button (Figure 4.18B). The line from the current column onwards will be spoken as long as the button is held down, so that she hears 'only runbs one program'. She therefore moves the taso further to the right until she hears another high-pitched beep. Pressing it for a short time, she hears 'runbs', confirming that she has located the right word. She moves the taso a little to the right, so that she hears another (lower pitched) beep (Figure 4.18C). Pressing the taso button will now cause the word to be spelled out, 'r u n b'. So, by moving through three more beeps the user moves the speech cursor to the extra letter. She presses the button to check (Figure 4.18D). Now the user must move the text cursor to the speech cursor, which she can do with the +7 command, as described above. She deletes the letter, and the exercise is complete.

Having a separate speech cursor with its own controls obviates the need for a browsing mode of operation. This makes it much easier to scan and read the screen contents, but, as illustrated by the above example, it also makes interaction with the application more difficult.

Kurzweil Personal Reader

The Kurzweil Personal Reader often seems to be the ideal example of modern technology being used to alleviate the effects of a disability: if people cannot read books because they cannot see, then devise a machine to read the books for them. Though it seems an obvious idea, it is not more prevalent mainly for practical reasons: it is very difficult for a machine to read print.

There are two phases to the operation of such a machine: reading the print text in and essentially translating it into text (this stage is known as **optical character recognition**, or **OCR**) and then converting that text into speech. The latter, text-to-speech operation is discussed more fully in Chapter 2, but it is the inputting of the print text which is the more difficult problem. Given the ability to read, human readers have very little difficulty in deciphering a wide range of formats of text and so may not realize the complexity of the task. The first problem is the range of different typefaces and sizes which are used. To a human reader it is quite obvious that the two samples in Figure 4.19 are the same yet it is very difficult to programme a computer to recognize the similarity. A human reader takes in the whole word as a pattern, but if you look at the

AllgTH   AllgTH

Figure 4.19   Letters which can look very different in alternative typefaces.

AIIgTH   AIlgTH

Figure 4.20   The letters in Figure 4.19, enlarged.

magnified letters in Figure 4.20, you get a view more analogous to that which is presented to a computer.

The first obvious difference is that the letter g is quite different in the two samples. Though the Ts are similar the one on the right has little serifs attached to the ends of its crossbar and at the end of its foot. The As are completely different. What is it that makes a letter recognizable as an A? The one on the left has two parallel vertical lines connected at the top by a horizontal bar with another horizontal bar across halfway up. That middle bar is about all that this A has superficially in common with the right-hand one. It has no vertical bars (but two angled ones) and no horizontal top bar. In fact the A on the left is very similar to the left-hand H, with just the top horizontal bar missing, yet there could be no confusion between the A and the H on the right. Even greater confusion is likely between the capital I and lower-case l in the left-hand sample. In fact there is visually no difference between them. They can be distinguished only in context. Effectively what the reader (be it human or computer) has to decide is: Is there a word with an I in that position?

These examples are relatively simple. They do not include variations of size or style (such as italics). The example also assumes that the printing of the letters is perfect – which is often not the case in practice. Printing ink on paper can be quite haphazard, and using photocopies or typewritten script is subject to even greater variation.

This description should give an impression of why it is so difficult to get a machine to read printed text. By extension it should be clear also why machines cannot read handwriting – even relatively uniform printed text is difficult enough.

Another serious obstacle to accurate optical character recognition is the different page layouts which can be used. Pages may have one, two or more columns – or even combinations. As an example of a difficult form of text to read by machine, take a look at a newspaper. An article may have a headline in a large typeface extending over perhaps two column-widths. The first paragraph or two may be in a bold typeface and also extend over two columns. Then the typeface may get smaller and continue down just the leftmost column. At some point that column terminates (probably above the headline for a separate article) and the reader must locate the continuation of the article somewhere above in the next column. Again, this processing is relatively simple for a human reader, who has a good high-level overall view of the text, but difficult for a machine reader which is essentially working at a microscopic level.

The description above has emphasized how difficult automatic interpretation of printed text is. However, it has been achieved. A greater obstacle is the interpretation of pictures. The Kurzweil Personal Reader basically gives up if it encounters a diagram. It will generally recognize the presence of a diagram but can make no attempt to interpret it. If a picture truly is worth a thousand words it should be apparent that even human readers transcribing books on to audio tape have an almost impossible task if they try to describe diagrams aurally. Allowing access to graphical information to blind people remains a challenging research question.

Despite all the difficulties of the task, as described, the Kurzweil Personal Reader achieves a very high level of accuracy at reading printed text, making it a realistic means of gaining access to some text. Yet it is not a panacea; it is not a universal answer to the problem of giving blind people access to printed text. The principal limitation of the Kurzweil Personal Reader is its cost. Given the difficulty of its task, a great deal of expensive development has gone into the production of quite specialized hardware. It must be said, though, that the cost has come down dramatically over the years. When first introduced in the late 1970s it cost around £40,000, while at the time of writing (1990) the cheapest version (the 7315 Model 10) costs about £8,000. This still means that it is not practical as an item to be owned and used by an individual, but is rather confined to being available in libraries and institutions.

Another problem – as with most speech devices – is the quality of the speech. If a person wishes to read a whole book, or even just a significant proportion, it may be quite tedious to hear it all in synthetic speech. The latest version (the 7315 range) does use the Dectalk synthesizer, giving it about the best quality of speech currently available – and a choice of nine different voices. This means that at least users can vary the voice over a long reading, and that they can use different voices to distinguish the text being read from system messages.

Access to printed material is provided for many blind people through audio tapes. That is to say, human readers read the material and record it on to cassette tape. This does provide the material in a human voice with natural intonation (though the intonation may still leave a lot to be desired, especially if the material is of a technical nature outside the experience of the reader). In most countries such a tape-reading service is available on demand – but not instantly. If a blind person requests a title that has not been recorded already there may be a delay of several weeks before a recording can be supplied. Such a delay may be frustrating for the client and the work can be all wasted because, having received it, he or she may realize that the text was not what was expected. In other words, a reading machine gives instant access to a book, and allows the possibility of browsing.

As illustrated in Plate 4, the Kurzweil Personal Reader has four principal components: an electronics unit, a keypad, a hand-held scanner and a table-top scanner. The electronics unit contains all the essential hardware components, including the synthesizer. It can be used in conjunction with either of the scanners. The table-top scanner is very similar to the scanning mechanism of a photocopier. The text to be read is laid face-down on a glass plate and a lid closed over it. A mechanically driven optical system then scans the text and transmits the information to the electronics unit for translation into speech. The hand-held scanner performs the same operation, but instead of the scanning being carried out automatically by a mechanical device, it is up to the user to move a small camera over the text. It is important that the camera is moved accurately along the lines of text, and this could obviously be a difficult operation for a blind person to perform. However, the hand scanner is used in conjunction with a magnetic tracking aid which is placed under the text. The paper can be placed quite accurately on the tracking aid, under a clipboard-like clamp, and movements of the scanner are then confined magnetically to a horizontal direction. In this way the user can scan a line of the text. Once that line has been successfully read, the scanner can be moved down to the next line, but that takes a certain amount of extra force, which the user perceives as a distinct 'click'.

Plate 4   Raymond Kurzweil pictured with his invention, the Kurzweil Personal Reader.

Obviously the table-top scanner is easier to use in that it obviates the need for the user to do the scanning. However, the hand-held scanner is much more portable. The electronics unit is designed to be portable (it has a carrying handle) and carrying it is much more feasible without the table-top scanner. Another advantage of the hand-held scanner is its low cost, a difference of around £2,000.

As with all the technology examined in this book, a vital feature is how the user can control the speech. In other words, the human–computer interface is critical. Control is effected via the eighteen-key keypad. Because of the power and flexibility of the Personal Reader, the control facilities are extensive, so that the keypad operates in four modes:

1. Reading mode;
2. Setup mode;
3. Communications Setup mode;
4. Calculator mode.

Reading mode is the default one, and the one through which users can interact with the document they are reading. Setup mode allows users to vary the style of the speech, to select which voice should be used, for instance. An important feature of the Personal Reader is that it can be linked to other computers, so that it can store and load text from them. There is a variety of ways in which computers communicate (compatibility problems again) and the Personal Reader's Communication Setup mode allows the user to match it to different computers. Calculator mode is a little curious in that it turns an expensive, powerful reading machine into a talking calculator – equivalent to one which could be bought for a few pounds (see Appendix A).

One key which is common to all keypad modes and always in the same position is the NOMINATOR key. This enables the user to identify any key. If the user presses the NOMINATOR key and then another key, the second key's command is not executed, but its name is spoken. Some keys control a menu of options. For instance, reading can be line-based or sentence-based. Pressing the SENTENCE MODE key will cause the Reader to say 'Sentence mode is on'. Releasing the key at that point will leave the Reader in sentence mode, but pressing it again will elicit 'Sentence mode is off', as indeed it will be.

When reading text, people do not simply start at the beginning and read on to the end in a single scan. People often need to re-read sentences or glance backwards and forwards in the text. This is obviously true when examining a reference book, but it is also the case when reading a narrative, such as a novel. The blind user of a Personal Reader must have the possibility of controlling the reading in the same manner. This is done through the keypad, in Reading mode.

A piece of text is scanned by the Reader, translated into the internal computer code (as described above) and is then stored in the Reader's memory. Associated with that text in memory is a conceptual marker, which indicates the current place in the text. The marker moves through the text as it is read, and the user has the option of moving the marker backwards and forwards.

The simplest way to read through a document is to use the NEXT SENTENCE key. If the Reader is in sentence mode, the marker will move in units of sentences, otherwise it moves in lines. Holding the key down will cause all the text to be spoken out. To have the last sentence repeated the listener would release the NEXT SENTENCE key and press the LAST SECTION key. Speech can also be paused or terminated mid-utterance, by way of the STOP AND CONTINUE key. Other keys enable the user to move around the text in units of words or characters.

At any time the user can hear a spoken message summarizing the current status of the Reader, by pressing the STATUS key. This is available in all modes except Calculator mode, and reports information such as whether sentence mode is on. It is also the means by which the user can be informed when an error has occurred.

As well as the speech, the Personal Reader uses a variety of beeps, generally as a means of confirming that some action has occurred. There is a simple broad encoding, whereby high-pitched beeps signal some normal event, mid-pitched ones indicate an error and low-pitched ones indicate a serious error.

The style of the speech is controlled through the Setup keypad. The Personal Reader uses the Dectalk synthesizer, and so has its selection of voices available, which the user can choose through the READING VOICE CONTROL key. One good feature is that the user can specify that the text should be read in a different voice from error messages. As well as changing the voice, the user can also control the tone of voice, from a flat monotone to a highly animated tone (judged to be 250 per cent of the normal level of animation). Most importantly, speed can also be altered, and the speed of speaking words can be controlled independently of the speed of spelling letter by letter. Word rates of 120 to 350 words per minute are available.

The Personal Reader has a finite amount of memory. If someone is going to re-read a book many times they may prefer to scan it in once and then store the computerized text. To do that he or she will have to connect a computer to the Reader and make use of the computer's memory – usually its disc on which the document can be stored long term. Communications have to be configured through the Communication Setup keypad, but once the compatibilities have been resolved it is a relatively simple matter to transfer scanned texts on to the computer – and to copy them back. This allows the user to re-read a book very quickly because the document need not be re-scanned and scanning can be very time-consuming.

Transferring a text to a computer does also offer the possibility of processing it. In particular, the scanner is not perfect and sometimes introduces errors. By word processing the text on the computer, the user can manually correct such mistakes.

The foregoing description of using the keypad may make it sound very complex. The modal operation of the keypad entails the danger of users losing track of what mode the system is in at any time. For instance they may think the keypad is in Reading mode and press the LAST LETTER key, but if the mode is actually Setup then it will be the READING VOICE CONTROL key that they have pressed, and the identity of the current reading voice will be spoken instead of the last letter. Of course, the NOMINATOR key helps users to avoid such errors.

Despite the complexity, users seem to find it quite easy to learn. This is due to a number of factors. There is a good degree of consistency between modes, such as the position and function of the NOMINATOR and STATUS AND MESSAGE keys. At the same time, the four modes are quite separate and the user is rarely likely to have to switch frequently between modes. For instance, the user will use the Setup modes only occasionally; once the speech and communications setting have been chosen they can be stored and should not need to be altered, so the user will operate almost exclusively in Reading mode.

The Personal Reader would seem to be an almost ideal application of technology. It provides a solution to a difficult problem, giving one way of overcoming a major handicap associated with blindness – lack of access to text. Of course it is not an ideal or a complete solution: reading is not perfect, mistakes are made and diagrams are quite unreadable; the Reader is expensive and not very portable. However, the Kurzweil

Personal Reader has already shown a significant improvement in these areas over the past few years, and we can only expect further improvement. There is a question as to how much need there will be for reading machines in the future when books may be available in forms other than on paper. This idea is pursued further in Chapter 6.

Summary

This chapter has described important examples of speech-based technology which is already available commercially. We now go on to look more toward the future. The screen reader programs described above are inadequate to deal with modern computers with graphical user interfaces and this is the topic of the next chapter. Finally, in Chapter 6 we look further into the future and predict what is likely to be the outcome of today's research.

Further Reading

Edwards and Grove (1988) describe the Voice screen reader. This is an experimental system which is quite similar to Hal but was intended to overcome some of the shortcomings of existing screen readers. In particular, it better handles the use of **bit-mapped** characters (see Chapter 6). It also has a more consistent set of commands and an extensive help facility. It also has the attraction of being available at no cost.

National Braille Press (1987) reviews a large number of screen readers, mostly available for PC and Apple II computers.

Woltosz (1988) provides a description of the Equalizer, as used by Stephen Hawking.

5 Adapting Graphical User Interfaces

Introduction

The screen readers which are described in the previous chapter are designed to give access to computer screens which display information in a textual form. The description of text-to-speech translation has shown that it can be difficult, but technology has been developed which achieves it quite well. The major challenge in designing such systems is, therefore, providing the **user** with good control of the speech. Such systems all rely on the fact that the computer presents its information in a textual form which can be translated into synthetic speech. The major contemporary challenge in this area is posed by the adoption of human–computer interfaces which display information in a non-textual format, which is not amenable to translation into speech.

As described in Chapter 3, a great deal of effort has been expended on making computers more accessible to a wider range of users through improving the human–computer interface. The major resultant development has been interfaces which are not based just on textual information. Specifically there has been the development of the graphical user interface (GUI). In addition to the keyboard, which was previously used as the means of communicating to the computer, GUI systems have a pointing device (usually a **mouse**) which can be used to point at, and interact with, visual images on the computer screen. Windows, icons and menus are categories of the images used in such interfaces. Figure 5.1 shows a typical screen on such a system and Figure 5.2 is a legend of the symbols on the screen.

A mouse has one, two or three buttons on its top surface which can be activated by the user's fingers. Pressing a button is usually referred to as 'clicking'. Many interactions are performed by moving the mouse such that the cursor points to a chosen object on the screen and then a mouse button is clicked. In Figure 5.1 the cursor has been moved to the head of the File menu and then a mouse button pressed and held down. Another form of interaction is achieved by clicking the mouse quickly twice in one spot. This is referred to as 'double-clicking'. A third form of interaction is the 'drag', whereby the marker is moved to point at an object, the button pressed and held down. Then, with the button still depressed, the mouse is moved to a new position.

The cursor gives the user continuous positional feedback. The basic skill required of

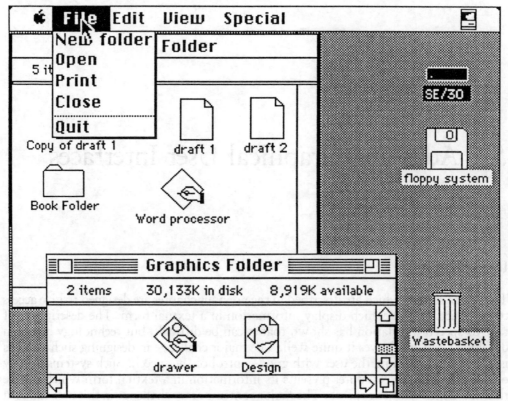

Figure 5.1   A typical screen of a graphical user interface.

the user in using the mouse is hand–eye (or visual–motor) co-ordination. As the mouse is moved, the user receives feedback about the position of the pointer on the screen relative to the items displayed on it. The user is almost entirely dependent on the (visual) information of the position of the cursor. Although users can also see the position of the mouse and sense its position through their muscles that information is of less value.

It must be recognized that, although the mouse is an input device, it is intimately associated with the computer output. Contrast the mouse with a keyboard: a keyboard is an input device, and a touch-typist can use a keyboard without receiving any output feedback from the computer. (Indeed, this is how many blind typists work on conventional typewriters.) However, no one can use a mouse without receiving some form of feedback (output) regarding the current state of the cursor.

Graphical user interfaces have become very popular, mainly because they make the computer much more accessible to novice users. Because the interaction is not limited to the communication of just text in both directions (i.e. input from a keyboard and output print on a screen) it has been possible to incorporate interactions which resemble activity in the everyday (i.e. non-computer) world, and which reduce the load on the user's memory. Commonly such interfaces are based on the metaphor of the desk top. For example, a word-processed document might be represented as an icon representing a piece of paper (e.g. the icons DRAFT 1, COPY OF DRAFT 1 and DRAFT 2 in Figure 5.1). To

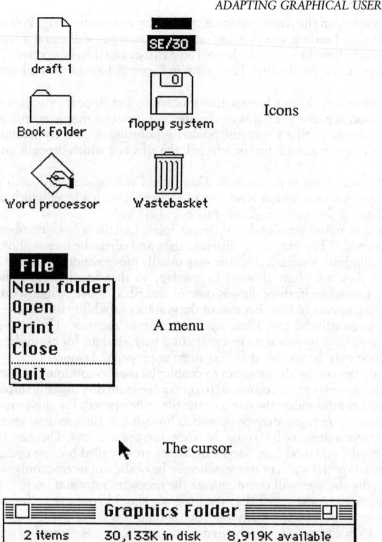

Icons

A menu

The cursor

A window

Figure 5.2   A legend of the symbols on the screen in Figure 5.1.

obtain a printed copy of the document, the user might use the cursor to drag its icon over to another icon resembling a printing machine, and, for deletion, drag it to another icon representing a wastebasket. This style of interaction seems easier to most novice users.

Menus generally come in one of two varieties: pull-down and pop-up. A pull-down menu has a fixed location on the screen, which is marked by a menu heading. Pointing the mouse cursor at that heading and pressing one of the buttons will cause a list of menu entries to appear below the heading. One of those entries can then be selected. The effect of so doing depends on its identity. The menus in Figure 5.1 are of the pull-down variety.

Pop-up menus, however, do not have a fixed location, but appear wherever the mouse is when a button is pressed. That is to say, the user presses a mouse button and a menu appears, positioned so that the mouse pointer is pointing at an entry within it. Once again, one of those entries can then be selected, the effect of which depends on its identity.

Another style of screen item is the *button*. This should not be confused with the buttons on the mouse. A screen button is an area of the screen with a label which will have a particular effect if the cursor is pointed to it and clicked.

Windows are used in many ways and in different roles. Usually a large number of windows may be opened. They may be of different sizes and often the user is allowed to alter the size of a window. Similarly, the user may usually move windows around the screen. Furthermore they are often allowed to overlap, so that manipulating them effectively becomes a problem in three dimensions. As described above, windows may be used to display the contents of files. Because of the graphics capability of the screens, the files need not necessarily be text files, but may contain pictures. The program controlling the window may format data in a particular way, so that, for example, the contents of a **database** may be displayed as text in an appropriate layout.

Some windows are opened by the program to enable the user to communicate with it. For example, if the user executes a command to open a file from disc (usually through a menu) the user must communicate the name of the file to be opened. For this purpose a *notification window* or *dialogue* may be opened. Through this the user may specify the name – possibly from a menu or by typing the name into the window. There are two forms of dialogue: modal and modeless. Modal dialogues are so called because opening one puts the user into a special state, or mode, whereby he or she can interact only with the dialogue. Normally the user will communicate the necessary information (e.g. the appropriate file name) and then signal that the program should continue, using that information. However, one button in any dialogue should always allow the user to cancel the command which opened it in the first place, in case it was opened in error. Modal dialogues are used when the program cannot continue without further information from the user. So, in the above example of opening a file the dialogue would be a modal one since the program could not complete the open command without the file name. The user would specify the chosen name and then signal that the program should continue, in which case the appropriate file would be opened. If the open command had been selected in error, then the user would cancel the dialogue (by clicking on a cancel button, as illustrated in Figure 5.4) and no file would be opened.

From the description above it should be quite clear that modern GUI-based systems are extremely visual, and hence are likely to be very difficult to adapt for use by people who cannot see a screen. However, though it may be difficult, it is imperative that means are found of providing such adaptations. Scadden (1984) points out that many visually disabled people have been enabled by the use of information technology to attain a degree of equality in job opportunities in areas involving the use of that technology, such as word processing. Yet there is a definite rapid spread of systems with interfaces that are complex visually. For instance, another author has suggested that, 'The future lies with a graphical windowing interface, mouse cursor control, pull-down menus, dialog [*sic*] boxes, and the like', and that computers based on such interfaces 'are destined to take over the IBM PC and compatible world, as well' (Zachmann, 1987, pp. 13–14). At the same time Scadden (1984, p. 399) warns, 'If such visually-oriented computer equipment were to become dominant in the microcomputer marketplace, blind and visually impaired people would lose much of the newly acquired equality, unless . . . alternative approaches were available.'

If Zachmann's premise is accepted and it is assumed that visually disabled people are to continue to be able to use information technology, ways must be found of making highly visual interfaces accessible to them. In a company which uses **PCs**, with their text-based interface, blind workers can be accommodated through the provision of screen readers, but if that company should then decide to standardize on new GUI-based systems, what will happen to their blind employees? This is not an imaginary scenario; it has already occurred. As Bowe (1987, p. 55) has stated, 'When Drexel University required all its freshmen to buy Macintosh computers . . . it was sending the message that "no blind person need apply here".' Further impetus has been added to work on this problem by the passing of the US legislation on accessibility of computers, mentioned in Chapter 3.

This chapter describes two attempts to address this problem. The first is embodied in Outspoken, which essentially extends the synthetic speech screen reader to the graphical user interface. The second approach has been tested by implementation in a **word processor** called Soundtrack.

Outspoken

Outspoken is a commercially available adaptation for the Apple Macintosh. It makes the system and **applications** accessible through the use of synthetic speech. It is entirely implemented in **software** and is installed simply by copying one file on to the user's disc. Outspoken uses the Macintalk software speech synthesizer (which will also have to be copied on to the disc if not already there).

Outspoken gets round the problem of a blind user guiding the mouse around the screen by avoiding its use. All mouse actions are replaced by keyboard commands and the mouse cursor serves as the speech cursor also. These are generated by the numeric keypad which is standard on Macintoshes. Figure 5.3 shows the keypad, labelled according to its use with Outspoken. The most used keys are UP, DOWN, LEFT and RIGHT, which move the cursor as appropriate within its current context. Notice that these keys are arranged in a cross pattern, their position corresponding to their action. The user does have the option of using the mouse, but this would be very difficult for a blind person.

Operation of Outspoken can be illustrated by way of a similar example to that used in the previous chapter, but extended to illustrate how it copes with the difficult problems of icons and windows. Assuming that the user starts as in the earlier examples, she launches the word processor with the required document. As before, she wishes to search for a particular word. There is a FIND command in the word processor's Edit menu. Outspoken (see below) does allow the user to access commands in menus.

Figure 5.3   The Macintosh keypad as used in Outspoken.

However, Macintosh applications have *keyboard equivalents* for the most commonly used commands. These are specified using a **modifier key**. This is very similar to the control key on other keyboards, but is called the 'Command' key, and is marked by the special symbol ⌘ .

The word processor has a search command which is evoked by typing ⌘-F. This opens a dialogue through which the user will specify the word to be found. When the dialogue opens, Outspoken announces 'Dialogue'. The user types the target word, which is pronounced by Outspoken, and then presses the RETURN key on the main keyboard. The first occurrence of the target word is highlighted in the document window. However, the Find dialogue is essentially another window and it has become the active one. To examine the occurrence of the word in the document the user must make its window the active one. To do that, she presses the WINDOW key (Figure 5.3). This makes Outspoken open what is essentially a *pop-up* menu – which is *not* a part of the standard interface. Outspoken says; 'Windows menu'. By pressing the DOWN key the user hears the names of each of the windows. By pressing SELECT when she has heard the name of the document window, the user activates that window. She must now move the cursor to the target word.

The above procedure may sound complex, especially as it will have to be repeated if the occurrence of the word found is not the correct one (except that the target word will not have to be re-typed – the search command will 'remember' the most recent target). The example does however illustrate some of the operations involved in using Outspoken.

Fortunately, the designers of Outspoken have built in a much simpler find command. The user would proceed as follows. She would press the SCROLL key on the keypad, followed by the FIND key (Figure 5.3). She must then enter the target word, terminated by a RETURN. She is now in a position to explore the text surrounding that word. Pressing RIGHT causes the words to the right to be spoken, and similarly for LEFT. Having decided that this is not the required occurrence of the word, she can search for it again by pressing SCROLL, FIND, RETURN. As in the previous example sessions, the user decides she needs to explore the paragraph further this time. Pressing UP causes the current line, up to the selection, to be spoken. Pressing it twice again causes Outspoken to read the previous two lines. The user now decides to hear those lines in the right order, so she presses DOWN three times.

Having decided that this is the paragraph preceding the point at which a new paragraph should be inserted, the user searches for the end of it. She can listen to each line, using the DOWN command as before. She does not have to listen to every word. Once she has heard enough of one line pressing DOWN will interrupt the current speech and start the next line immediately. Having located the appropriate position, she must select that point, by pressing SELECT and she then types in the new paragraph. When she types slowly, each word is spoken, but if she increases her speed, they are not spoken.

Having entered the paragraph, the user proofreads it. She uses the UP and DOWN commands, as before. Having located a line in which she suspects there is an error, she uses RIGHT to move along word by word to the erroneous one. By then pressing SPELL that word will be spelt out. To delete the extraneous letter it must first be selected, so the user holds down the SHIFT key and presses RIGHT, which moves the cursor letter by letter. The simplest way to delete the extra letter is to move the cursor to the right of it, press SELECT and then press the DELETE key on the main keyboard. Nothing is spoken when DELETE is pressed, but the user can check that she has deleted correctly by pressing SPELL again.

To quit the word processor, there is a keyboard equivalent available (⌘-Q). It will request whether the user wishes to save the document to disc first, through a dialogue. This poses the question, 'Do you want to save file?' and has three buttons, YES, NO and CANCEL (see Figure 5.4). Again Macintosh software has a convention which allows one to use the keyboard. The default button in a dialogue (which in this case is YES) is executed if the user presses RETURN. However, let us suppose that this time the user decides she has not made all the changes she wants, and so she wishes to abort the quit command. She must move to the dialogue and locate the CANCEL button. To move to

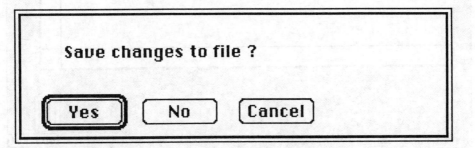

Figure 5.4   A dialogue which the user might have to access through Outspoken. The items marked YES, NO *and* CANCEL *are* buttons.

the dialogue she must use the WINDOW key, as before. Once in the dialogue, pressing DOWN makes Outspoken read out 'Do you want to save file?', and pressing it again makes it read 'Button, yes. Button, no. Button, cancel'. The user can 'home in' on CANCEL using RIGHT and then execute it with the SELECT key.

One of the attractions of word processing on computers such as the Macintosh is that it offers a variety of typefaces, sizes and styles. Suppose the user decides to change the typeface of the whole of this document. She must first select the whole document. There is a keyboard equivalent to do this, ⌘-A. To choose the new typeface she must, however, use a menu. She presses the MENU key. This moves the cursor to the left-hand end of the menu bar (Figure 5.1). There is always a special menu in that position, marked by an apple symbol, so Outspoken says, 'Menu apple'. Pressing RIGHT moves the cursor along the menu bar, reading out the menu titles thereon. The required one is called FONT. Once that is located, the user presses the DRAG/RELEASE key. This causes the menu to be pulled down, revealing a list of the available fonts. The user moves down that list and hears the names of the typefaces. When she hears the name of the required one, she presses DRAG/RELEASE again. This will have the desired effect of changing the typeface in the document. Now the user does quit the word processor, as outlined above.

Suppose the user changes her mind completely about what she has just typed, and

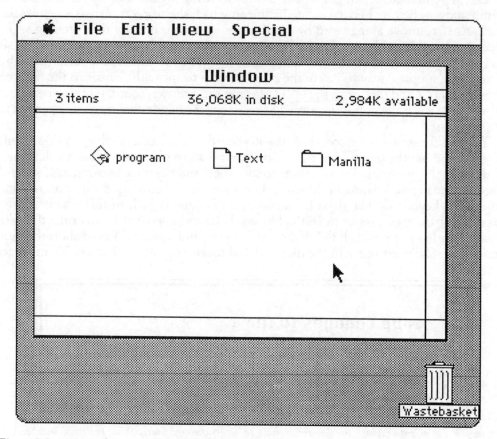

Figure 5.5   A typical screen which might have to be interpreted through Outspoken.

wants to discard the document. On the Macintosh the only way to remove a file is to drag its icon on to a special 'Wastebasket' icon. To do this the user selects the appropriate window. She can explore that window, using the directional commands. So, for instance, DOWN would 'describe' the top row of the window in Figure 5.5 thus: 'Icon program. Document text. Folder manilla.' The user could locate the appropriate file in this manner, or by using the FIND command. She then presses DRAG/RELEASE to select the icon. She must then press the WINDOW key. Always at the bottom of the window menu is a special entry, Desktop. This refers to the screen area which is the background to all the windows. The user selects this and presses RIGHT. This moves the cursor to the Wastebasket, which is signalled by Outspoken saying 'Wastebasket', and it drags the file icon with it, so that by pressing DRAG/RELEASE once more, the file is dropped into the wastebasket, and hence removed.

Although Outspoken uses mostly speech, it does also make use of other simple sounds. A particular 'beep' signals 'no more', such as at the edges of the screen and the bottom of a menu. Text documents on the Macintosh usually display a flashing selection marker, and in Outspoken this is also represented audibly as a clicking sound. Various other beeps are used to signal different factors – which ones depending somewhat on how the user has set up Outspoken for her own use. There is another sound associated with dragging. As long as an item is selected for dragging, that sound is heard.

Outspoken is a significant development and an excellent contribution to solving a real and difficult problem. Its importance is discussed further below, but it does leave one difficult problem outstanding, that of how to adapt non-textual, graphics programs.

Soundtrack

Soundtrack represents a rather different approach to the same broad problem as that addressed by Outspoken, though the shorter-term aims of this project were somewhat different. First, the intention was to explore some possibilities as to how graphical user interfaces might be adapted for blind people; it was not an attempt to provide a generalized adaptation. Similarly, since it was the principles which were being explored, it was important that they should not be too specific to any one computer or system. It was also decided that the mouse should not be replaced.

Given these aims, principles were devised whereby graphical user interfaces might be translated into an auditory form. The principles were then tested by incorporating them into a program and that program was evaluated with the assistance of a number of visually disabled people. The first design principle was that items which a sighted user sees on a screen should be replaced by items which can be *heard*. The design of the resultant auditory interface also had to be constrained in order to reduce its complexity. As far as possible, the auditory items were as close as possible as analogies to their visual counterparts.

A word processor was chosen as an application which would be the basis of the test software as it would be relatively easy to evaluate, with the aid of visually disabled people who were already familiar with word processing. It is worthwhile stressing that this project was *not* an attempt to create a better word processor for blind users; the word processor was a vehicle through which the ideas of an auditory interface could be investigated. Soundtrack was implemented on an Apple Macintosh computer. It was written in Object Pascal. Speech is generated using the Macintalk software speech synthesizer.

For the sake of this investigation, certain constraints were applied to the design which might not be desirable in a real production program, but which tested the limits of the design. For instance, as far as possible standard **hardware** was used, so that the adaptation was embodied entirely in software. Similarly, it was decided that the interface should be entirely auditory, even though a better interface might be devised which also made use of tactile communication.

Because blind users are expected to use the mouse, they need constantly available spatial cues. For that reason Soundtrack makes much more use of non-speech sounds than Outspoken does, as explained blow. The interface is constructed from *auditory objects*. An object is defined by the following properties:

● its spatial location;
● a name;
● an action;
● a tone.

One constraint applied was that objects cannot overlap. Their arrangement is therefore based on grid arrangements. Two forms of sound are used in the interface: musical tones and synthetic speech. Broadly speaking, tones are used to communicate imprecise information quickly and speech is used to give more precise information more slowly. Additionally, speech is used to communicate the contents of documents being processed. An object's tone is sounded when the mouse is moved to point to it and the name of

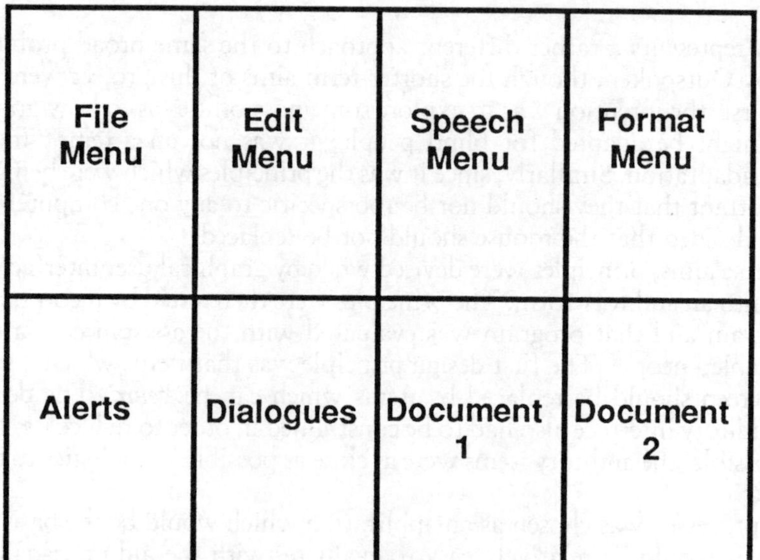

File Menu	Edit Menu	Speech Menu	Format Menu
Alerts	Dialogues	Document 1	Document 2

Figure 5.6   Soundtrack's auditory screen, a grid of auditory windows.

the object currently pointed at is spoken if the user presses the mouse button. (The Macintosh mouse has a single button.)

The pitch of the tones varies with position, rising from left to right and bottom to top. Several different types of tone are available, and can be selected by the user. The default type is based upon sine waves and in addition to variations in pitch it makes use of chords, in a manner which is described below. The edges of the screen are marked with another, distinctive tone.

Auditory objects are structured into two levels. At the upper level, the user interacts with an *auditory screen* comprising eight *auditory windows*, as illustrated in Figure 5.6. As the user moves the mouse across window boundaries their tones are sounded, and their names can be ascertained, as described above.

Auditory windows are used as a means of grouping related components of the interface and each one of them has a fixed position on the screen and a particular role. To progress to interacting at the second level, the user *activates* a window, by moving the cursor into that window and then double-clicking the mouse button. Activation causes the window to become subdivided into a set of component objects. For instance, the activated File menu window is illustrated in Figure 5.7. The same protocol applies within an activated window, so that each (sub-)object has a tone and a name which are produced as described above. The principal type of component object within windows is the *button*. Double-clicking, or 'executing', a button causes its associated action to be carried out by the application.

The tones for the component items of an activated window are single sine-wave tones. Their pitch varies in the same way as described for the auditory screen, rising (in major thirds) as the mouse moves from left to right and bottom to top. It was mentioned earlier that chords are used. An unactivated window's tone is a chord consisting of the tones of its component items. The root of the chord is the note assigned to the bottom leftmost component item and the root notes of horizontally adjacent windows rise in major seconds.

As users move the mouse around a number of different sounds are generated, giving

Figure 5.7   The activated File menu. Visually it resembles a menu on a standard, visual program, but it is also defined by sounds.

an impression of the contents of the screen. Moving the mouse horizontally they will hear a gentle rise in pitch, while if they move vertically they will notice a greater jump (a fifth, to be exact). At the same time, if they move into a window such as the File menu which has a large number of component items they will hear a rich chord, whereas if they move into a window which is empty (as the Alert window is most of the time) they will hear just a single tone.

The operation of Soundtrack and the use of some of the other windows shown in Figure 5.6 can be described through a short example of creating a new document. To create a document the user must firstly locate and activate the File menu. The user would then locate the 'New' entry within the menu (Figure 5.7). Executing that entry causes a document effectively to be displayed in the Document 1 window. To type into the new document the user would first move the mouse out of the (still-active) File menu and over to the document window, which he or she would activate. The user could now type text into the document and each word typed would be spoken back (under default conditions).

The document windows represent the furthest deviation from a direct analogy with visual interaction in Soundtrack. Operations in visual word processors apply to a portion of the text, which is said to be 'selected' and which is identified by being highlighted on the screen. Soundtrack maintains the concept of a selection, but differs in the manner by which the selection is controlled. In a visual word processor the contents of the document are displayed in a window and the user specifies the selection by pointing at it directly. In Soundtrack a document window consists of a set of buttons which control the selection (see Figure 5.8).

The counterpart to the highlighting of the selection in Soundtrack is for it to be spoken in synthetic speech. At any time each document has a *level* setting, corresponding to one of the following units:

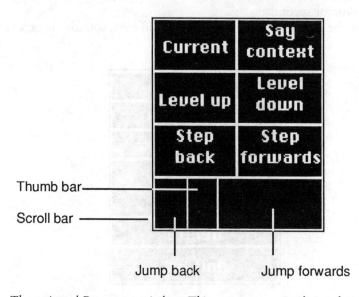

Figure 5.8 The activated Document window. This represents a significant deviation from a direct analogy of anything in a visual word processor.

- the whole document;
- paragraph;
- sentence;
- word;
- character;
- the point between two characters.

For example, if the current level is 'word' and the user double-clicks on the STEP FORWARDS button then the selection will move to the next word. The new selection is spoken whenever it is changed and the user can hear the current selection at any time by double-clicking on the CURRENT control. The setting of the level is controlled by the LEVEL UP and LEVEL DOWN controls. The selection is adjusted accordingly (and spoken) as the level is altered and the user can ascertain the current level of a document by clicking once on the CURRENT control.

The JUMP controls enable the user to move the selection in larger units. Whereas the STEP controls move the selection in units corresponding to the current level, the JUMP controls operate at the level above. That is to say, for example, that if the level is 'character' and the user executes a JUMP FORWARDS, the selection will move forward to the first character of the next *word*.

The SAY CONTEXT control enables the user to hear the text surrounding the current selection without altering the selection. Executing it causes the text at one level up to be spoken. For example, if the level is 'word', SAY CONTEXT will speak the sentence containing the selected word.

The thumb bar is one object which is not a simple button. It works by moving the selection through the document, the selection's position corresponding to the relative position of the thumb bar within the scroll bar. For example, if the current level is 'paragraph' and the thumb bar is moved to its leftmost extreme, then the *first* paragraph in the document will become selected. The user receives auditory feedback as to the current horizontal position of the thumb bar in the form of intermittent tones, which increase in the frequency with which they are sounded from left to right.

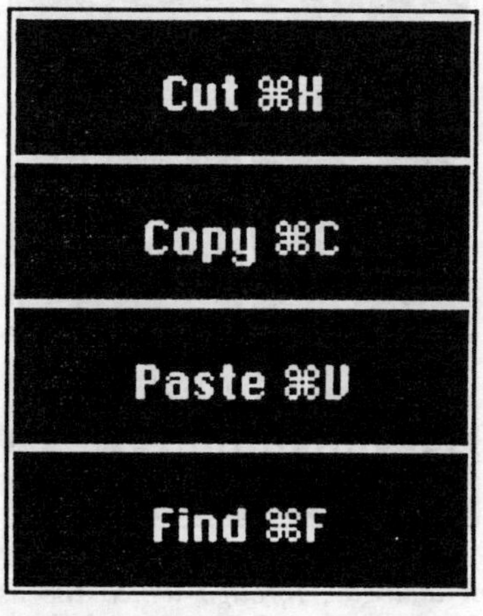

Figure 5.9   The activated Edit menu.

Editing operations act on the current selection, as in a conventional word processor. So, for instance, to delete a word the user would select it, using the operations described above, and then execute the CUT command, which is in the Edit menu (see Figure 5.9).

Having completed the editing operations, the user would close the document by executing the 'Close' entry in the File menu (Figure 5.7). At that point a decision must be made as to whether the document should be saved on disc. This would be ascertained through the Dialogue window. This window is used whenever the program needs further information from the user. In this case the window would be filled with the Save file dialogue illustrated in Figure 5.10. This dialogue is *modal* in that the user cannot activate any other window and so is forced to respond to the dialogue. Should the user execute the YES button, the program would then obtain a name for the new file by way of another dialogue. The Alert window is used in a similar way to the Dialogue window but it signals errors. The roles of the other windows are described in Edwards (1987), along with more complete description of this project.

Notice that the descriptions given above are expressed entirely in terms of the interaction between the mouse and sounds generated, which is the fundamental form of the interface. Blind users will perceive the interface entirely through these interactions and for their purposes nothing need be displayed on the computer's screen. In practice, the state of the auditory screen can be reflected on the visual screen, in a form similar to Figures 5.6–5.10. This has the practical benefit that a blind user can obtain help if needed from a sighted colleague. This is also an example of *redundancy* in the interface. Such redundancy is not only likely to make the program easier to use, but it also makes it more easily adaptable to users with different needs.

It is imperative that any innovation, such as Soundtrack, should be evaluated by people who might use it; there is a danger in developing an aid for people with a disability in that the (usually non-disabled) developers produce what *they think* those people need, rather than what they actually need. Therefore Soundtrack was evaluated with the aid of seven volunteer visually disabled subjects. The evaluation was by way

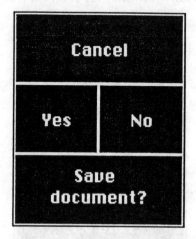

Figure 5.10   *The Save document dialogue, through which the user specifies whether the current document should be saved to disc. Compare with the 'standard' visual dialogue in Figure 5.4.*

of a small-scale feasibility study: to see whether the design principles applied in Soundtrack were likely to form the basis of usable interfaces.

The evaluation was based upon teaching subjects to use Soundtrack by leading them through a set of graded exercises. The subjects' views of using Soundtrack were obtained through structured interviews, based on a questionnaire, which were carried out once they had completed their training exercises. Other data were obtained while they were carrying out exercises. An added feature of Soundtrack was that it could be made to record all the user's interactions (movements of the mouse, presses of the mouse button, presses of keys, etc.). These records were saved in a file which could be later analysed by another program. This facility was used to obtain data on the time subjects took to complete certain tasks. It was also used to record their behaviour in carrying out fairly complex word-processing tasks – those which came late in the graded set. These log records were supplemented by audio recordings of the dialogue between the subject and the tutor and the two were combined in written transcripts.

One important aspect of using a computer system is the time taken to perform tasks. Timings recorded during the evaluation exercises were used to explore one of the novel interactions incorporated in Soundtrack: the location of auditory targets by the mouse. As mentioned in Chapter 3, designers of visual interfaces can use Fitts's law to predict users' pointing performance and the measurements made in this evaluation resulted in a model which could be used in a similar fashion for auditory interfaces.

It should be stressed that this is only a *model*. It is not a law, with the same generality as Fitts's law. It applies only to the auditory protocol implemented in Soundtrack, and not necessarily to all users. For instance, one subject used the pitch information to locate objects in such a way that his behaviour did *not* fit into the model.

The major feature of the pointing model is that location times are comparatively slow. The major component of the time turns out to be thinking time. This includes the time the user takes to choose the target and to plan how to move to it. The model can be used to compare the performance of Soundtrack with other programs. This would be applicable to comparisons with other programs designed to be used by blind people and with unadapted visual software. It could also be used as a means of identifying bottlenecks in its use and so to improve its design. The figures obtained suggest that Soundtrack is significantly slower than a comparable visual word processor.

Broadly, the conclusion of the evaluation was that Soundtrack was a usable program, but that there were difficulties in using it. Opinions varied as to what was the most difficult aspect of using Soundtrack, but most of the problems seemed to be associated with the limitations of the user's memory, and in particular the need to recall the layout of the internal structures of the windows. All the subjects used verbal techniques (mnemonics) to remember the arrangement of the windows within the screen, but none of them had an explicit internal representation of the objects within any of the windows. It seems that the memory load, and particularly the use of a verbal representation, is largely responsible for the slowness of the location times.

It was also evident that the simple tones of different pitch were of limited help to the users. Most of them did not use the pitch information, but simply counted the *number* of tones sounded. The one notable exception was a subject who had a musical background and who used a very different strategy in locating objects on the screen (which did *not* fit the model of targeting), by listening for their tone.

These results suggest that there is scope to improve the interface by employing sounds which are more useful, which communicate more information to the average user, and hence reduce the memory load on the user.

All the subjects made the same comment that they would have liked to have had some form of physical frame in which to move the mouse. Some of their comments suggested that they found it somewhat unnerving to interact with an entity which was embodied entirely in sounds. This relates back to the earlier discussion of the suitability of the mouse. There are a number of problems in providing such a frame. One is that it is possible for the pointer to get out of step with the cursor – as would happen, for instance, if the ball on the bottom of the mouse skidded on the desk top. Also, as described above, the contents of the screen and its windows change during use of the program and it would be difficult to reflect such changes in any physical (presumably mechanical) frame.

In fact, during the evaluation some of the subjects had experimented informally with using a graphics tablet and stylus in place of the mouse. This did form a simple frame including the use of a tactile overlay on the tablet, marking the outline of the auditory windows (similar to the illustration in Figure 5.6, but without the window labels). Reactions to the use of the tablet were mixed. Some of the subjects had dexterity problems in using the stylus, but most seemed to think that the tablet would be better if they had had time to become accustomed to it. Two of them commented that it did provide a form of frame. One did make the point that he preferred not to use the tablet since it was not part of the standard hardware. There is a need for experiments to be carried out to determine the best form of pointing device for blind users of auditory interfaces. It may well be, for instance, that using a puck and tablet would have overcome the dexterity problems of the stylus and that such an absolute pointing device would have been more appropriate.

Part of the evaluation interview endeavoured to depersonalize the subjects' responses by asking them how long they thought it would take someone else to learn to use Soundtrack and what the minimum necessary level of previous experience would be. Two considered that no related experience was necessary, but the remainder agreed that trainees should at least be able to touch-type. Several of the responses to questions regarding the training of other would-be users appear to reflect subjects' frustrations regarding the form of training they had received. Estimates varied widely as to how long it would take a trainee to become proficient at using the program, but there was general agreement that training sessions should be closely spaced. This is in contrast with the evaluation exercises, which were usually weekly. Several of the subjects suggested that trainees would learn to use the program better if they were given time to experiment with it on their own. This response probably was partly a reflection of the fact that the subjects' access to the program had been limited and controlled, due to logistical limitations.

The Significance of Outspoken and Soundtrack

A limitation of Outspoken is that it is a very specific product. It runs on only one computer (though the choice of the Macintosh is a courageous one as it has become something of the *bête noir* of blind computer users), but furthermore it has had to be written in an non-standard manner, such that it cannot be guaranteed to work with future versions of the hardware or the system software. In particular, within a year or so of Outspoken's release, Apple was planning a major upgrade in its system (from Version 6 to 7). Though only time and the release of Version 7 will tell, it seems unlikely that Outspoken will run at all with the new software. This is not a criticism of Outspoken as such. It merely illustrates that computer manufacturers do not pay sufficient regard to the need of all potential users, for if they did, an adaptation such as Outspoken would be capable of being implemented without the programmer having to resort to non-standard 'tricks'.

In the long run, the greatest contribution of Outspoken and Soundtrack is that they should help to guide manufacturers as to how they ought to design their systems. In the shorter term it is too early to judge whether Outspoken will persuade blind users to use Macintoshes. It does make some things possible which were not before (access to a wide range of Macintosh software for blind users), but that may still be too difficult to make users move from their tried and trusted PC-based systems – yet. Eventually it must happen one way or another because graphical user interfaces are here to stay for the foreseeable future.

Remaining Research Questions

The development of auditory interfaces for blind users is a relatively new field of investigation. The principal conclusion from the work reported is that there is a great deal of scope for further work. The Soundtrack project was modest in its aims: it tested the feasibility of adapting interfaces into an auditory form. Though its results do seem to support the feasibility they also suggest that there is a lot of work to be done before this kind of adaptation will become generally useful.

Redundancy is a very important part of human communication. This is illustrated by the fact that many people dislike using the telephone because they lose many of the redundant visual cues which are available in face-to-face communication. Yet redundancy is almost completely absent in current human–computer interfaces. Generally, the computer reacts to interactions in a visual manner, and the user who misses the visual effect will miss the event completely. There is a case, therefore, for redundancy to be introduced into interfaces, so that visual events might be accompanied by an auditory signal. This is the focus of other work in this area but also has implications for disabled users, who often rely on signals which are redundant to able-bodied communicators. A deaf person, for instance, may use the visual information of lip, tongue and body movements to read speech. Building redundancy into human--computer interfaces will make adaptation easier, or even unnecessary. For instance, one of the features of Soundtrack is that there are two representations of the screen. Everything which occurs on the auditory screen is also reflected on a visual screen. This does imply that the program could be used equally by people who are blind, able-bodied or even deaf.

The development of graphical user interfaces has been based upon graphics display technologies. This has further implications for adaptation for blind users. Most of the screen readers mentioned in Chapter 4 rely on the fact that the contents of the screen are stored in **memory** as **ASCII** characters. The screen reader can ascertain the contents of the screen by examining that area of memory. However, in graphics displays using **bit-**

mapped technology the identity of individual characters is lost, and representations of characters will be interspersed with non-alphanumeric information, such as icons and other graphical items. One screen reader, Voice (Edwards and Grove, 1988), has been developed which will read bit-mapped displays, but this is a very specific solution which will work only on the MS-DOS^{TM} operating system.

At this point, pending further research, it is possible only to speculate on the sorts of sounds which will be used in auditory interfaces for blind users in the future. To what extent will work on use of sounds in interfaces for sighted users be relevant to blind users? On the one hand, apart from vision the relevant abilities of blind users (cognition, hearing, etc.) can be assumed to be the same as other users. On the other hand, their need for an entirely non-visual interface means they will have different requirements of sounds.

One approach which is suggested for incorporating sounds into visual human–computer interfaces is based on the use of natural sounds. For instance, when a file is deleted, by having its icon dropped on to the icon of a waste bin there is a crashing sound of rubbish being thrown into a bin. This approach may be quite appropriate in some cases for blind people who are familiar with sensing the world largely through hearing. Also, the amount of learning required is an important factor and such *everyday* sounds should take less time to learn. Yet since the blind user may be reliant entirely on auditory information complex messages must be passed, which might be beyond what can be captured in such natural sounds. This complex information should be encodable in a more symbolic but less natural form.

The meaning of sounds which are symbolic has to be learned. A blind person may be willing to invest some more effort into learning to use a system with an auditory interface because there is no alternative accessible interface. However, that does not mean such an interface will be adopted regardless of how difficult it is to use. Using any device is an investment and people will use a product only if they perceive that the pay-off in terms of usefulness to them is worth their investment of effort in learning to use it and actually using it. The low number of blind braille-readers is an example of this. Even the chance to access vast amounts of literature is not sufficiently motivating to make most blind people want to make the effort to learn braille. It is therefore imperative that blind people are involved in the design and evaluation of any innovation intended for their use.

It was pointed out earlier that there are two possible approaches to providing access to computers for disabled people: custom-building applications and providing adaptations to existing applications. Although the Soundtrack project may appear at first sight to be an example of the former, it was carried out rather more with the latter objective in mind. (Recall that Soundtrack incorporated auditory components which were as closely analogous as possible to visual counterparts.) The results of the project suggest that if one wanted to develop a better interface for blind users one would probably discard the mouse altogether. However, the suggestion is that commercial computer interfaces for the foreseeable future will incorporate a mouse, and if blind people want to play their part in that world then ways of adapting such interfaces must be found. This is a more difficult problem and the most promising avenue for development seems to be the use of user interface management systems (UIMSs, see Betts *et al.*, 1987). A UIMS offers multiple representations of the user interface, and it remains to be seen whether one representation might be an auditory one. In other words, it might be possible to have one application with two interfaces, one auditory (suitable for blind users) and one visual (suitable for everybody else).

One aspect of interface design which has been highlighted by the Soundtrack project is how developments which benefit some users are to the detriment of others. To be more specific, the development of GUI-style interfaces has made systems easier for sighted people to use – including some people with motor impairments who find it difficult to use older keyboard-based interfaces. Yet those same developments have made interfaces more difficult to adapt for visually disabled people to use. It has been said that it is the decisions which designers make when they are *not* thinking about the needs of disabled users which have the greatest effect on disabled people. It is to be hoped that in the future the needs of disabled users will be considered as part of the normal development of interfaces, rather than an 'optional extra', added on at a later stage. The current American legislation is an encouraging step in this direction.

This chapter has illustrated how the development of visual user interfaces has led to the use of displays of information in forms other than text and that, consequently, adapted auditory interfaces must exploit sounds in a more imaginative manner. In particular, synthetic speech alone is not sufficient. Soundtrack represents an early, tentative move in that direction. It is by no means the only possible approach and the results of its evaluation strongly suggest the need for significant further work in the area.

Further Reading

The journal *Human–Computer Interaction*, Vol. 4, no. 1 (1989) is a special edition on the use of non-speech audio in the interface. It includes a paper by Gaver, who advocates the use of everyday sounds in the human–computer interface, and one by Blattner, Sumikawa and Greenberg proposing a structured form of symbolic sounds. Further details of Soundtrack can also be found in Edwards (1987).

6   The Future

Looking Ahead

Unless you are the possessor of special powers and a crystal ball, predicting the future is a hazardous exercise. This is particularly true in the rapidly changing and evolving field of information technology. The potential use of synthetic speech by people with disabilities has been realized for as long as people have been trying to generate synthetic speech, but was it envisaged as being used in the way that it is, and what can we say about how it will be used in future? In the 1960s, when digital technology was just beginning to become established, did anyone foresee the sort of products discussed in Chapter 4?

A machine which can read books might have appeared in science fiction. Communicators for people who lack the power of speech would have been a fairly obvious prediction, but the means of accessing it was probably not even thought about a great deal. In the 1960s and 1970s the number of people using computers was still small, and the idea of individuals owning their own computers seemed unlikely, so there was no need for blind people to have access to them.

One constant trend throughout the development of speech synthesis has been the improvement in speech quality and this can only continue; the quality available now is far better than twenty years ago, but there remains so much scope for improvement. As suggested earlier, the ultimate objective would be voices of quality which communicator users would be proud to use, which they would have personalized to suit their own self-image.

Current Research

Clues as to what the future may hold may be found in the laboratories, today's research which should bear fruit tomorrow. This section outlines some current research topics and projects in various related areas.

Speech Synthesis

Articulatory synthesis may be one technology which will lead to better quality in the future. There is as yet no significant slowing down in the increase of computer power and decrease in the price of the technology, which should also contribute to improvements in speech quality. For instance, diphone-based synthesis is another technology which is being developed, and as **memory** becomes even cheaper it will become more feasible to store larger numbers of more precisely recorded diphones.

A Music Manuscript Processor

The development of word processors with speech output has provided numerous blind people with an independent means of writing. Similar independence has been sought by blind composers for the preparation of music manuscripts (scores). For those people who currently prepare music in braille, it requires a sighted person with knowledge of both braille and conventional music notation to provide transcription between the two media.

The techniques that have been successfully used for word processing have been applied to music. The problem is greater because of the graphical nature of music where the location of notes, and other features, has a significant musical meaning. Conventional music manuscript-writing **software** is usually dependent on graphical displays which can be manipulated with a cursor.

A trial music manuscript processor has been developed at the Open University for the BBC Master microcomputer. It is based on a talking **word processor** model with pitches, note values and duration entered as codes that have musical significance, with the 'bar' being an identifiable unit for placement and editing. The techniques adopted proved to be acceptable to the composers involved in the evaluation. However, limitations in the memory size of the computer restricted the introduction of some essential features such as beaming and slurs.

More recent developments have attempted to add a screen reader to standard manuscript writing software. Although direct access to graphics features has not been possible, the use of word-processed files that contain codes which, in turn, can be edited and transferred to the standard software for printing the manuscript, has provided another option. This achieves high-quality music representation but not all the speech techniques that are desirable can be introduced compared with those in a customized speech output program.

Input Technology

It has already been pointed out that a vital requirement is for faster input techniques. The current research on Chat at Dundee University was discussed in Chapter 3. Recall that so far Chat handles only the opening and closing smalltalk of a conversation, and as yet skirts the more difficult, less predictable information exchange of the main section of a conversation. Hopefully, the lessons learnt so far will be extended and applied to more general conversations.

Another prototype product from Dundee is Pal. This is input software which cuts down on keyboard keystrokes by predicting the **user's** input. As the user types the first few letters of a word, Pal will present options as to what the word might be, which the user can accept with a single keystroke. Pal keeps track of the words used by an individual, so adapting to his or her vocabulary. Rates of keystroke reduction from 30–60 per cent have been recorded.

A very different approach to the input problem is not to use any kind of keyboard. Input devices have been developed based on the recognition of hand *gestures*. One form of gesture is sign language, and researchers in California have developed the Talking Glove, which recognizes signed English and finger spelling and converts it into synthetic speech (see Kramer and Leifer, 1987). This has a number of attractions. It allows the user to communicate in their 'first' language with people who do not know that language. It can be used by someone who cannot type (though some forms of manual impairment obviously might preclude both typing and signing).

Other experiments with gesture-based input have concentrated on non-sign-language gestures. Instead they get the user to control the parameters of the (synthetic) speech through gestures – rather as natural speakers control their speech through the bodily movements within the vocal tract.

Topics for Further Research

The previous section described some of the research currently under way. There are other areas which have not yet been investigated but which clearly need to be better understood if the best use is to be made of speech synthesis. This section describes some of them.

There is a question as to how much need there will be in the future for reading machines (such as the Kurzweil Personal Reader), which will be correlated with the extent to which paper-based documents continue to be used. Much has been made in the past of the so-called 'paperless office' in which all documentation has been moved on to the computer. However, so far this idea has proved to be fallacious; anyone working in an organization with many computers is more likely to confirm that his or her office is in fact deluged with paper print-outs, generated with great ease by the computer. However, increasing amounts of information are being held on computers which could be made more accessible to people via their own computers. In particular, many books (including this one) are written on word processors. The word processor file is used to typeset the printed book, which is the form in which the book is distributed.

It is ironical that a blind person may have to spend a great deal of money and time on a Personal Reader, which is used to translate the printed book *back* into a computerized (machine-readable) form. It would seem that it would be much better if the book could be distributed on a disc which the user could have read directly. Currently, the major problem with this idea is that publishers are very reluctant to release books in this format because computer data are so easy to replicate that free copies of the book could be readily made and distributed.[1] It is only to be hoped and expected that such obstacles will become less of a problem in the future. Already there are moves in the right direction in that the Next computer is supplied with the complete works of Shakespeare and *Webster's Dictionary* on its large-capacity optical disc. This is not to suggest that books will be completely replaced by electronic media. Bound, paper books have qualities of their own which will be a long time dying in people's affections.

Software is needed which will allow the user suitable access to the text. The user will require the same sort of access facilities as provided by the Kurzweil Personal Reader. As illustrated in Chapter 4, these facilities are very similar to those provided by the combination of a word processor and screen reader, which might provide good, if somewhat makeshift access. However, there is scope for the development of much more extensive means of browsing through documents. It ought to be possible to give blind users a level of access at least equivalent to that of a sighted reader of a printed book, but it may actually be possible to give them *better* access. This remains a current research topic.

A related topic for further research is how to deal with diagrams. The Kurzweil Personal Reader simply gives up if it encounters a diagram. In most cases it will announce that there is a diagram present which it cannot interpret. An even more challenging problem is that of allowing blind computer users to create diagrams. There have been some experiments with using non-speech sounds to represent simple diagrams (Mansur, Blattner and Joy, 1985). This approach may be combined with software which has more **artificial intelligence** built in, in the form of rules which describe how graphical items interact. The program might be able to interpret aspects of diagrams, and this might be expressed in speech, as well as guiding the user in creation and exploration of the diagram. Research into this area is as yet at a very early stage.

Dreams?

Imagine you are having a conversation with an expressive synthetic speech user of the future. The first thing to notice is that you do not even realize that the individual is not using his or her own voice. He or she looks and sounds like anyone else. The voice is right for the person's appearance and character – because he or she designed it that way. There is no slow keyboard or switch for input, because input to the synthesizer is generated by a brain implant reading patterns. In other words the speech is composed in the head, much as everyone else does. And the speech does not come from some electronic speaker, but out of his or her mouth. Where better to put the (highly miniaturized) synthesizer?

What kind of adapted human–computer interface will the blind computer user of the future be using? None. All such interfaces will be based on multiple media, just as

---

[1] These fears do have some foundation. The novelist Douglas Adams writes his books on a word processor. He sent a copy of one of his books to his American publisher on a floppy disc. Somehow a copy of that file found its way (illegally) on to a computer network. Thereafter any subscriber to the network could print out a copy for little more than the price of the paper – even before the published version had been released.

human communication is. As well as the visual component there is an auditory one – and a tactile one. For most users the diversity of the communication merely adds to its richness and naturalness. The sighted user is aware of the auditory and tactile components but does not appreciate that it is possible to perform the same interactions using only those media, without the benefit of the visual channel. Many symbolic sounds are used, but at certain levels of communication, speech is still a vital component of the auditory interface.

Are those scenarios far-fetched? Possibly, but in the 1960s, when computers cost millions and filled rooms, who would have dared to suggest that blind people would ever even need access to them, or that talking computers would become small enough and cheap enough to be used as a substitute voice? There is no reason to suppose that the basic technology will not continue to develop rapidly; all that is needed is the realization of its usefulness in the forms described in this book, and for that to be backed up by research and the necessary financial support. Such research must be seen not as a minority interest, but as part of the mainstream. It will not only be of benefit to users with disabilities, in addressing their special needs, but will also feed into more general research on human–computer interaction for all users.

Having read a book like this, one should not be blinded into assuming that the development of information technology is always to the benefit of disabled people. For instance, earlier chapters included accounts of ways of adapting computers for blind users. However, the adaptations are not universal. They do not make all computers and all programs accessible. Hence, moving some forms of work and education on to computers may exclude people from those opportunities. There is, therefore, no room for complacency. On balance information technology will be of benefit to disabled people only if their needs are constantly borne in mind. It is the decisions which designers make when they are *not* thinking about the needs of disabled users which usually have the greatest effect on them.

Further Reading

Computer Bulletin (1988) briefly describes Pal and Chat.

References

Allen, J., Hunnicutt, M. S. and Klatt, D. (1987) *From Text to Speech: the MITalk System*, Cambridge University Press.

Alm, N., Arnott, J. L. and Newell, A. F. (1989) Discourse analysis and pragmatics in the design of a conversation prosthesis, *Journal of Medical Engineering & Technology*, Vol. 13, no. 1/2, pp. 10–12.

Arnott, J. L. (1987) High-speed control of a speech synthesiser by stenotype keyboard, *Proc. European Conf. on Speech Technology*, Vol. 1, pp. 335–8.

Arnott, J. L. and Newell, A. F. (1984) Stenotype shorthand and speech synthesis in vocal prosthesis for the dexterous speech impaired, *Proc. 2nd Int. Conf. on Rehabilitation Engineering*, pp. 621–2.

Atal, B. S. and Schroeder, M. R. (1970) Adaptive predictive coding of speech signals, *Bell System Technical Journal*, Vol. 49, pp. 1973–86.

Atal, B. S. and Hanauer, S. L. (1971) Speech analysis and synthesis by linear prediction of the speech wave, *Journal of the Acoustic Society of America*, Vol. 50, no. 2, pp. 637–55.

Baecker, R. M. and Buxton, W. A. S. (1987) *Readings in Human–Computer Interaction: a Multidisciplinary Approach*, Morgan Kaufmann, Los Altos, California.

Betts, B., Burlingame, D., Fischer, G., Foley, J., Green, M., Kasik, D., Kerr, S. T., Olsen, D. and Thomas, J. (1987) Goals and objectives for user interface software, *Computer Graphics*, Vol. 21, no. 2, pp. 73–8.

Bolinger, D. (1972) Accent is predictable (if you're a mind-reader), *Language*, Vol. 48, no. 3, pp. 633–44.

Boubekker, M., Foulds, R. and Norman, C. (1986) Human quality synthetic speech based on concatenated diphones, *Proceedings of the 9th Resna Conference, Minneapolis*, Minnesota, pp. 405–7.

Bowe, F. (1987) Making computers accessible to disabled people, *Technology Review*, Vol. 90. no. 1, pp. 52–9.

Bruckert, E. (1984) A new text-to-speech product produces dynamic human-quality voice, *Speech Technology*, January/February, pp. 114–19.

Card, S. K., Moran, T. P. and Newell, A. (1980) The Keystroke-Level Model for user performance with interactive systems, *Communications of the ACM*, Vol. 23, pp. 396–410.

Card, S. K., Moran, T. P. and Newell, A. (1983) *The Psychology of Human–Computer Interaction*, Lawrence Erlbaum Associates, London.

Carlson, R., Granström, B. and Hunnicutt, S. (1982) Bliss communication with speech or text output, *Proc. Intl. Conf. on Speech and Signal Processing*, ICASSP-82, pp. 747–50.

Carroll Center for the Blind (1983) Voice output for computer access by the blind and visually impaired, a special issue of the *Aids and Appliances Review*, issues no. 9 and 10, the Carroll Center for the Blind, 770 Carroll Street, Newton, Massachusetts.

Chomsky, N. and Halle, M. (1968) *The Sound Pattern of English*, Harper & Row, New York.

Computer Bulletin (1988) Computers as an aid to those with speech impediments, *Computer Bulletin, Awards Supplement*, p. iii.

Downton, A. C., Newell, A. F. and Arnott, J. L. (1980) Operator error performance and keyboard evaluation in Palantype machine shorthand, *Applied Ergonomics*, Vol. 12, no, 2, pp. 73–80.

Edwards, A. D. N. (1987) Adapting user interfaces for visually disabled users, unpublished Ph.D. thesis, Open University.

Edwards, A. D. N. (1989) Soundtrack: an auditory interface for blind users, *Human–Computer Interaction*, Vol. 4, no. 1, pp. 45–66.

Edwards, A. D. N. and Grove, P. (1988) *A User's Guide to the Voice Screen Reader*, Open University Centre for Information Technology in Education, Technical Report no. 57.

Edworthy, J. and Patterson, R. D. (1985) Ergonomic factors in auditory systems, in I. D. Brown (ed.) *Proceedings of Ergonomics International 85*, Taylor and Frances, pp. 232–34.

Elovitz, H. O., Johnson, R., McHugh, A. and Shore, J. E. (1976) Letter-to-sound rules for automatic translation of English text to phonetics, *IEEE Transactions on Acoustics, Speech and Signal Processing*, Vol. ASSP-24, no. 6, pp. 446–59.

Fairhurst, M. C., Bonaventura, M. and Stephanidis, C. (1987) Human–computer interaction in the provision of an interpersonal communication mechanism for the nonvocal, *Int. J. Man–Machine Studies*, Vol. 27, pp. 401–12.

Fawcus, M. (ed.) (1986) *Voice Disorders and Their Management*, Croom Helm, London.

Fitts, P. M. (1954) The information capacity of the human motor system in controlling the amplitude of movement, *Journal of Experimental Psychology*, Vol. 47, no. 6, pp. 381–91.

Gaver, W. (1989) The SonicFinder: an interface that uses auditory icons, *Human–Computer Interaction*, Vol. 4, no. 1, pp. 11–44.

Gray, D. B., LeClair, R. R., Traub, J. E., Brummel, S. A., Maday, D. E., McDonough, F. A., Patton, P. R., and Yonkler, L. (1987) *Access to Information Technology by Users with Disabilities: Initial Guidelines*, General Services Agency, Washington DC.

Hawking, S. (1988) *A Brief History of Time, from the Big Bang to Black Holes*, Bantam Books, London.

IEEE (1969) IEEE recommended practice for speech quality measurements, *IEEE Transactions on Audio and Electronics*, Vol. AU-17, no. 3, pp. 225–46 (also published as IEEE Standards Publication no. 297).

Isard, S. D. and Miller, D. A. (1986) Diphone synthesis techniques, *Proc. IEE Int. Conference on Speech IO*, London, pp. 77–82.

Klatt, D. H. (1987) Review of text-to-speech conversion for English, *Journal of the Acoustic Society of America*, Vol. 82, no. 3, pp. 737–93.

Kramer, J. and Leifer, L. (1988) The talking glove: a communication aid for deaf, deaf-blind, and non-vocal individuals, *Rehabilitation Research and Development Center 1988 Progress Report*, Veterans Administration, Palo Alto, California, pp. 123–24.

Mansur, D. L., Blattner, M. M. and Joy, K. I. (1985) Soundgraphs: a numerical data analysis method for the blind, *Journal of Medical Systems*, Vol. 9, no. 3, pp. 163–74.

May, J. G. (1982) Speech synthesis using allophones, *Speech Technology*, April, pp. 58–62.

Murray, I. R., Arnott, J. L. and Newell, A. F. (1988) Hamlet – simulating emotion in synthetic speech, *Proc. Speech '88*, Edinburgh, pp. 1217–23.

National Braille Press (1987) *The Second Beginner's Guide to Personal Computers for the Blind and Visually Impaired*, 2nd Edn, National Braille Press, Boston, Massachusetts.

Newell, A. F. (1986) Communicating via speech – the able bodies and the disabled, *Proc. IEE Int. Conference on Speech IO*, London, pp. 1–7.

Patterson, R. D. (1982) *Guidelines for Auditory Warning Systems on Civil Aircraft*, Civil Aviation Authority, CAA Paper 82017.

Poulton, A. S. (1983) *Microcomputer Speech Synthesis and Recognition*, Sigma Technical Press, Wilmslow, Cheshire.

Roberts, T. L. and Moran, T. P. (1982) A methodology for evaluating text editors, *Proceedings of the Conference on Human Factors in Computer Systems*, Gaithersburg, Maryland.

Rowden, C. G. (1986) Barriers to the acceptance of synthesized speech as a communication aid, *Proc. IEE Int. Conference on Speech IO*, London, pp. 220–4.

Scadden, L. A. (1984) Blindness in the information age: equality or irony?, *Journal of Visual Impairment and Blindness* (November), pp. 394–400.

Scadden, L. A. and Vanderheiden, G. C. (1988) *Considerations in the Design of Computers and Operating Systems to Increase Their Accessibility to Persons with Disabilities, Version 4.2*, Trace Research and Development Center (address in Appendix B).

Schroeder, M. R. (1985) Linear predictive coding of speech: review and current directions, *IEEE Communications*, Vol. 23, no. 8, pp. 54–61.

Shearer, A. (1981) *Disability: Whose Handicap?*, Basil Blackwell, Oxford.

Smith, S. L. and Mosier, J. (1986) *Guidelines for Designing User Interface Software*, Mitre Corporation, Bedford, Massachusetts.

Sumikawa, D. A., Blattner, M. M., Joy, K. I. and Greenberg, R. M. (1986) Guidelines for the syntactic design of audio cues in computer interfaces, *Proc. Nineteenth Annual Hawaii Int. Conference on System Sciences*, pp. 691–99.

Teja, E. R. (1981) *Teaching Your Computer to Talk*, Tab Books, Blue Ridge Summit, Pennsylvania.

Tremain, T. E. (1982) The government standard linear predictive coding algorithm: LPL-10, *Speech Technology*, April, pp. 40–9.

Woltosz, W. (1988) Stephen Hawking's communication system, *Communication Outlook*, Vol. 10, no. 1, pp. 8–11.

Zachmann, W. F. (1987) *A Look into the Near Future – 13 Predictions for the World's Computer Industry*, International Data Corporation, Framingham, Massachusetts.

Glossary

Amplitude The maximum height of a waveform. See Figure C.1 in Appendix C. In the perception of a sound wave, amplitude corresponds to the quality of loudness.

Analogue See digital.

Application [program] Software is generally divided into two categories: system software and applications. System software comprises the programs which help to give the user access to the computer's facilities. It performs such roles as organizing files on discs and handling input and output. Whereas system software is concerned with running the computer, applications programs (or simply 'applications') comprise the tools which perform the tasks the user wants. So, applications include word processors, spreadsheets, drawing programs and suchlike. Applications run with the support of the systems software.

Artificial intelligence (AI) The branch of computer science which is concerned with making computers behave with human-like intelligence. The objective is to make machines react in a similar way to a person when confronted with a novel circumstance, without them having to be explicitly programmed to deal with all possible events. At any time in the development of computer technology, the term 'artificial intelligence' has been associated with whatever it is difficult to get computers to do at present. In the 1980s this included vision, speech understanding, problem solving and natural language translation.

ASCII American Standard Code for Information Interchange, though it is also a European, ISO, standard. This is a standard format for encoding text as numbers, which can be processed by computers. For example the letters A, B, C and D are represented as 61, 62, 63 and 64 respectively.

Bit A binary digit. This is the fundamental unit of information. If we know the result of an event with two equally probable outcomes (such as the tossing of a coin) we have one bit of information. A single bit is sufficient to represent all possible states of such an event. Conventionally the numbers 0 and 1 are used to represent bit values. More complex events require more bits. For example, if we want to be able to represent the days of the week we have a choice of one out of seven. We might use seven bits, the appropriate one being set to 1 and all others to 0, thus:

Sunday	0000001
Monday	0000010
Tuesday	0000100
Wednesday	0001000
Thursday	0010000
Friday	0100000
Saturday	1000000

However, since it is possible for a given day to have exactly one identity only, three bits are sufficient. Thus, the days of the week might be represented as follows:

Sunday	000
Monday	001
Tuesday	010
Wednesday	011
Thursday	100
Friday	101
Saturday	110

Memory is measured in bits and is often a limiting resource, so that using representations of information which minimize (e.g. three bits instead of seven, above) the memory requirement is usually important. Similarly, the rate of transmission of information can be measured in bits per second and is often a limitation of communications systems.

Broad-band noise   Sounds generally contain a range of frequencies. This is also true of other waveforms, including light. A pure sound, such as a flute, contains few frequencies, which corresponds to a pure colour. White light contains all frequencies and there is an analogous phenomenon in sound, known as white noise, which is perceived as a hissing sound, similar to that heard on an untuned radio receiver. A broad-band sound is similar to white noise, but without such a wide range of frequencies present.

Byte   A byte is a collection of eight bits. It is a convenient unit for measuring memory for several reasons, including the fact that one character (letter, number, punctuation, etc.) normally occupies one byte. Larger blocks of memory are often measured in kilobytes. One kilobyte is 1,024 bytes. Kilobytes are sometimes designated as kbytes, or often simply k, though beware that k is sometimes used to refer to 1,024 *bits*.

Database   A collection of interrelated data stored on computer so that it may be accessed and processed by users. Some large-scale databases are stored on mainframe computers dedicated to that purpose (e.g. company payrolls, airline reservations, etc.), but database programs are also available as applications software to run on microcomputers as just one of the programs available to the user.

Digital   Relating to the representation of quantities by digits. This is the representation used in computers because it is convenient to store digits in a binary form (see bit). Digital representations are discontinuous. For instance, if a quantity is being stored digitally as whole numbers, there is no way of representing a quantity of (say) $4\frac{2}{3}$. This compares with an analogue representation, which varies continuously with the quantity represented. (See also Chapter 2 on the digitization of sounds.)

Modern computers (and related equipment) are based upon electronic technology which handles digital data. It is therefore known as digital technology.

Frequency In perception of a sound wave, frequency corresponds to the pitch of the note. It is related to the wavelength: the higher the frequency the higher the pitch and the shorter the wavelength.

In visible light, different frequencies (wavelengths) are perceived as different colours. See also Appendix C, for a brief description of the physics of sound.

Function key Function keys are standard on PC-compatible keyboards (as well as many other computer keyboards). There are usually ten of them, designated F1 to F10. They do not generate characters and their significance depends on the software in use.

Hardware See software.

I/O An abbreviation for input–output.

Kbyte See byte.

Mainframe A large, powerful general-purpose computer. Its use implies a major investment of money and staff. This contrasts with microcomputers, which are inexpensive and normally used by individuals, but which are not as powerful.

Memory Unless specifically qualified, in this book memory refers to computer memory, not human memory. It is the component of the computer which is used to store data and programs. Cost of memory is a very important feature of any computer-based device, and cost is related to capacity (measured in bits or bytes) and how long it takes the device to access a piece of previously stored data. Memory is expensive, but balanced against cost is the speed – the time it takes to retrieve an item from the memory. Slower memory is less expensive, so most computers comprise a (comparatively small) amount of (fast) main memory, and larger amounts of (slower) secondary memory. There has been a dramatic trend during the development of digital technology for the cost of memory to decrease, so making the exploitation of more memory-intensive approaches viable. However, the general trends in price can be affected by non-technological, economic and political influences.

Main memory is built of chips, often (misleadingly) referred to as RAM or random-access memory. It is usually volatile, such that it loses its contents if the power is disconnected. Secondary memory is normally on discs, which are non-volatile.

Microprocessor See processor.

Modifier key A modifier key does not generate a character on the computer when it is pressed. Instead it must be pressed at the same time as another key and modifies the output from that key. The SHIFT key is a modifier key which is found on typewriter, as well as computer keyboards, and it makes a letter key produce the capital letter. However, computer keyboards also have other modifier keys. All computers have a CONTROL key (often written as CTRL) and standard PC-compatibles also have an ALT key. Pressing any key at the same time as the CTRL or ALT key produces a code distinct from any other one which can be generated on the keyboard. The significance of a CTRL or ALT code is determined by the software in use, but usually the keypress is not reflected as a character on the screen. Different conventions are used to express CONTROL and ALT codes, but in this book CTRL-X refers to the code generated if the control key is held down while the 'x' letter key is also pressed.

Mouse   A mouse is an input device for a computer. Mice vary in their design, but generally they consist of a small box, which fits comfortably into the palm of the hand and which is connected to the computer. As the mouse is moved around on a flat horizontal surface its motion is detected and reflected in movements of a pointer, or cursor, on the screen. If the mouse is moved to the right or left, the cursor moves to the right or left respectively. If the mouse is pushed away from the user, the marker moves up the screen and it is moved down the screen by pulling the mouse towards the user.

Mice usually have one, two or three buttons on their upper surface. Many interactions are performed by moving the mouse such that the cursor points to a chosen object on the screen and then a mouse button is pressed.

Noise   In communications, noise refers to unwanted signals which may detract from or mask parts of the salient signal, just as acoustic noise may make it more difficult to hear a person speaking.

Optical character recognition (OCR)   The operation of scanning printed text and converting it into a computer code, so that the information embodied in the text can be processed by the computer. This is the first stage of processing in a reading machine.

PC   Standing for personal computer, this acronym is normally reserved to refer to microcomputers of a particular design. That design was originated by IBM, but has been copied by most microcomputer manufacturers. They produce computers which are so similar to the IBM design that they can run all the same software, and so are said to be PC-compatible.

Peripheral device   The essential components of a computer are the processor and memory but they rely on other auxiliary components which are known as peripheral devices (or simply 'peripherals'). These include input/output devices such as terminals, printers and back-up memory such as discs and tapes.

Processor   The main components of a computer are: the processor, the memory and the peripheral devices. The processor is the central component, in which operations are applied to the data. Building a complete processor on a single chip – the microprocessor – was a major development in the history of computers as it opened the way to mass production and hence low costs.

Read-only memory (ROM)   Memory is generally available in two forms, read-only memory (ROM) and random-access memory (RAM). RAM is really misnamed; it is memory which can be altered by the computer. Information can be *written* to the memory and the same information subsequently *read* back at a later time. If new information is written to the same area of memory, it overwrites the original contents, so changing them. By contrast, ROM cannot be altered by the computer. In other words, it cannot be written to but only read from. The contents of ROM are loaded during manufacture and thereafter remain unaltered.

Real time This refers to the time scale of events in the physical world. This can be very different from the internal time scale within a computer, but sometimes they may have to be synchronized, in which case the computer is said to be working in real time. A typical example of a real-time system is an air-traffic control system, in which it is clearly critical that the computer's representation of two aircraft on converging courses keeps up to date with their actual relative positions.

Return One of the keys on any electric typewriter keyboard is the carriage return. The typist presses this at the end of a line of typing. This rolls the paper on one line and returns the paper carriage back to its left-hand edge, ready for the next line of typing. A similar key is also found on computer keyboards, but its name is often contracted to RETURN. In text-based applications such as word processors this key has a similar effect, but it is also used as a terminator of input sequences to the computer.

ROM See read-only memory.

Software Any computing system has two components: the software and the hardware. Broadly, hardware consists of electronic components including processors, memory and input/output (I/O) devices, while software comprises the programs which run on that hardware. The names derive from the fact that hardware tends to be fixed: its components are literally soldered together and so would be difficult to reconfigure. Software, on the other hand, is more ethereal and is capable of being modified by a programmer with relative ease.

Spreadsheet A software package widely used by managers and accountants.

User A generic term, usually short for 'computer user', though it may be more specific, referring for instance to a user of a particular computer or program.

Wavelength The distance between two corresponding points on a wave (see Figure C.1). The speed of a wave is constant, and the wavelength is related to the frequency by the simple formula:

$$wavelength = \frac{speed}{frequency}$$

See also Appendix C.

Word processor Word processing is the preparation of printed matter using automatic typewriting techniques. A word processor is essentially a computer confined to being used for this particular purpose. Often, though, computers run word processor applications software as just one of the programs available.

Appendix A   Equipment, Manufacturers and Distributors

Notes on Entries

It is not claimed that the list of equipment and manufacturers given is definitive or exhaustive. It represents a sweep of the most prominent available at the time of writing. Every attempt has been made to ensure the veracity of the entries, but no responsibility is accepted for any inaccuracies. This is a rapidly developing area and new products are being developed and released almost constantly. At the same time, being so volatile, some companies do not survive and products may become unavailable. Similarly, the prices quoted should be treated as a guide only. Remember, microelectronic technology tends to become cheaper, so current prices may be *lower* than those quoted! Prices given in dollars are US currency, unless otherwise stated. All prices are quoted exclusive of VAT and other additions such as shipping. Inclusion in this list does not constitute any form of endorsement by the author or publishers.

Anyone thinking of buying equipment is strongly advised to contact the manufacturer first. Independent advice is available through the organisations mentioned in Chapter I, the addresses of which are given in Appendix B.

Much of the material in this appendix is republished, with permission, from *Concerned Technology 1989: Electronic Aids for People with Special Needs*, by J. S. Sandhu and S. Richardson, published and copyright by the Handicapped Persons Research Unit, Newcastle upon Tyne Polytechnic, price £15.

Speech Synthesizers

Audiocard 300E   This is a copy-synthesis system, for use with IBM PCs and compatibles. It allows digitization and playback of arbitrary sounds – including speech. It comprises a short expansion circuit board, microphone, loudspeaker and software. The software is compatible with Turbo Pascal, assemblers, C and Basic.
Supplier   STC Mercator
Price   £299

Calltext 5000   This synthesizer takes the form of a slot-in card for IBM PCs and compatibles. It provides very high quality text-to-speech translation with three different male voices. It has a number of special pronunciation modes, such as letter by letter or abbreviation expansion.
Manufacturer   Speech Plus Inc.
UK supplier   Cambridge Adaptive Communications
Price $3,225

Calltext 5050   This synthesizer is an external version of the Calltext 5000 which connects to the computer through a standard RS232 port. An external speaker can be connected directly to the unit. It can be adapted to handle up to five channels of data input and output.
Manufacturer   Speech Plus Inc.
UK supplier   Cambridge Adaptive Communications
Price $3,900

Cricket   This synthesizer includes text-to-speech and natural voice capabilities, music, sound effects and a clock calendar. Included are a built-in speaker, volume control, headphone jack, power supply and tutorial manual. It interfaces to the Apple IIc through the modem port cable supplied. Software supplied includes demonstration and utility programs.
Manufacturer   Street Electronics Corporation
Price $180

Dectalk   One of the best-quality synthesizers currently available – with a price tag to match. It offers six different voices (male, female, child and adult). It accepts text from the host computer on a standard RS232 port and performs text-to-speech conversation including high-quality pronunciation and prosody. The rate of speech is adjustable from 120 to 350 words per minute. (See also Chapter 2.)
Supplier   Digital Equipment Corporation
Price $4,200

Decvoice   Decvoice is a complete speech technology device. It combines a text-to-speech speech synthesizer (Dectalk), a digitized copy-synthesizer and a speech recognizer. It is designed to work with a MicroVax™ workstation.
Supplier   Digital Equipment Corporation

Dolphin Mimic   A low-cost synthesizer of moderate quality. Superseded by the Dolphin Apollo, though there are a large number around within Britain.
Manufacturer   Dolphin Systems Ltd

Dolphin Apollo   A low-cost synthesizer of excellent quality for the price. It can be reconfigured for different languages; each unit can switch between two languages, and others can be enabled by replacement of a plug-in chip. The normal configuration speaks British English.
Manufacturer   Dolphin Systems Ltd
Price   £395

Echo   This speech synthesizer offers both unlimited vocabulary text-to-speech and more natural speech of canned text, in a plug-in board. Its text-to-speech system incorporates over 400 rules, providing intelligible but robotic speech. It can also be used to speak items from a fixed vocabulary (supplied on disc) in a natural-sounding female voice. It comes with an external speaker with volume control and headphone jack, a manual and speech utilities on disc.

Several models are available, compatible with different computers: Echo IIb (Apple II+, IIe and IIGS); Echo 1000 (Tandy 1000 EX and HX); Echo PC+ (IBM PC, XT, AT and compatibles); Echo+ (Apple II+, IIe – also features stereo music synthesis); Echo MC (IBM PS/2, models 50 and 60).

Manufacturer   Street Electonics Corporation
Price   In the range $120–180 (depending on model)

Echo Commander   A speech synthesizer designed to operate with the Apple II+, IIe and IIGS computers. This device allows many public domain and non-copy-protected programs to talk. The Echo Commander includes an interface card which plugs into one of the computer's expansion slots; an external speaker box with knob controls for rate of speech and volume and a headphone jack; a 5.25-inch floppy disc containing a specially modified version of Tex-Talker, a program which works in the background allowing other programs to speak; Tex-Talker documentation in large type, braille, and on the program disc along with printable instructions for the synthesizer.

Supplier   American Printing House for the Blind
Price $184

Macintalk   This is one of a new generation of synthesizers in that it is embodied in software, and relies on the standard sound-generation hardware built into the computer (the Apple Macintosh). It provides a good level of quality with some prosody. It is really intended for use by software developers and is *not* supported by Apple Computers. It comes with a set of utilities for creating and modifying exception dictionaries. (See also Smoothtalker.)

Manufacturer   Apple Computers Inc.
UK supplier   Apple Developers' Group
Price   £10 (note it is available only to members of the Apple Developers' Group)

Prose 2000 and 2020   A text-to-speech synthesizer for IBM PCs and compatibles. In addition to any ASCII text file the Prose 2000 will accept ASCII-coded phoneme codes for non-standard words and names. Other features: abbreviations, numbers and symbols are expanded to natural speech; high quality prosody, based on content and punctuation; speech output can be synchronized with other events; there are three male voices to choose from and the rate can be varied from 50 to 200 words per minute.

The synthesizer is packaged either as a slot-in board (the Prose 2000) or as a peripheral device (the 2020).

Manufacturer   Speech Plus Inc.

Slim   A speech synthesizer which is claimed to have a very high level of pronunciation and prosody. It can be used with IBM PCs and compatibles. It comprises an internal accessory card (with connections for a speaker and headphones) and an external speaker.

Manufacturer   Syntha-Voice Computers Inc.
Price $695 (Canadian dollars)

Smoothtalker   This is one of a new generation of synthesizers in that it is embodied in software, and relies on the standard sound-generation hardware built in to the computer (the Apple Macintosh). It provides a good level of quality with some prosody. It has a built-in pronunciation dictionary which can be modified by the user. It can be linked to programs written by the user to provide speech output. However, due to its copy-protection mechanism such programs are not portable. (See also Macintalk.)

Manufacturer   First Byte Inc.
UK supplier   MacSerious
Price   £49.95

Supertalker   This is a copy-synthesis system that can be used to add speech to applications on IBM PCs. Its hardware consists of an internal circuit card, a built-in speaker and a microphone. Phrases are spoken into the microphone and digitized for storage on disc. About 120 seconds of speech can be stored on a standard floppy disc. The software offers utility programs for adjusting how the sound is stored and for adding spoken phrases to application programs.

Manufacturer   Mountain Computer

Type 'n' Talk™   A phonetically programmable speech synthesizer, equipped with a standard RS232 serial interface. Features include: text-to-speech translation, 750-character buffer, adjustable pitch and volume.

Manufacturer   Votrax Inc.
Price $299

Votalker   The Votalker speech synthesizer provides four voice patterns through on-board switches. It has two pre-programmed voice modes that can be customized through a filter. It has a self-contained speaker, audio amplifier and external speaker jack. Two models are available, the IB and the AP, which plug into slots in IBM PCs and Apple computers respectively.

Manufacturer   Votrax Inc.
Price $249 (IB), $179 (AP)

Votrax   The Votrax™ Personal Speech System is a phonetically programmable speech synthesizer with a self-contained speaker and serial and parallel interfaces for connection to a computer. Features: unlimited vocabulary output, text-to-speech translator, user-defined exception word table, 256 programmable frequencies, 16 programmable amplitudes and speech rates, 3,500-character definable buffer, music capability, programmable clock with 8 definable speech alarms.

Manufacturer   Votrax Inc.
Price $449

PC Screen Readers

Artic Business Vision   A screen reader with conventional facilities. The system comprises a plug-in card, an external speaker, headphones and disc of software. The synthesizer offers four voices, independently stable for speed, pitch and tone.

Manufacturer   Arts Computer Products Inc.
UK supplier   Sensory Visionaid
Price   £486

Artic D'Light Business Vision   This is not just a screen reader, but is a package comprising the Artic Business Vision built into a Toshiba T1000 lap-top computer. It is available with the Turbo Pedal, a means of fast forward and rewind up and down text with pitch correction.

Supplier   Sensory Visionaid
Price   D'Light Artic £1,395
          D'Light Artic Business Version £1,495
          D'Light Artic Version with Turbo Pedal £1,605

Frank Audiodata   See Chapter 4 for a full description of this system.
Manufacturer   Frank Audiodata
UK distributor   Sensory Visionaid
Price   £3,250

Hal   A low-cost screen reader. It uses either the Dolphon Mimic or Apollo synthesizer. Control is based entirely on the keyboard, through ALT commands – some of which are not particularly memorable. It includes fairly sophisticated facilities for defining windows and such definitions can be stored on disc, so that the reader can be customized to work with particular applications. Probably the most-used screen reader in the UK.
Manufacturer   Dolphin Systems Ltd
Price   £395

Skerfpad   This is a screen reader which uses tactual information as well as speech. It includes a touch pad with an overlay of raised lines which represent the position of the lines of text on the screen. By pressing on the line the corresponding text is spoken. Skerfpad works in conjunction with either an Echo or Artic 200 synthesizer.
Manufacturer   Bill Loughborough
Price $250

Speaqualizer   A hardware-based screen reader. It consists of a full-sized card which will fit into an expansion slot in any IBM PC, XT, AT or compatible; a control box which houses the speaker, an earphone jack and a command keypad and connector cable. The manual is provided in braille and print.
Manufacturer   American Publishing House for the Blind
Price $780

Vert   Vert is available in two configurations and prices. At one extreme is Soft Vert, an entirely software-implemented screen reader which is also less expensive. It requires the addition of the synthesizer hardware, but that also means that the user has a choice of synthesizers. The more expensive version is Vert Plus, a hardware-based adaptation which involves the addition of a circuit card. It has the Calltext synthesizer built in. Vert Plus includes: software, speaker, headphones, plug-in board and documentation on disc, in print and on audio tape as well as a Quick Reference Guide in braille.

Vert is controlled through the standard keyboard. It has a simple programming facility so that its operation can be customized to match different applications.
Manufacturer   Telesensory Systems Inc.
UK distributor   Sensory Visionaid
Price   Vert Plus £2,995
          Soft Vert $495 (not sold in the UK)

Voice Voice is an experimental system which is quite similar to the Dolphin Hal, but was intended to overcome some of the shortcomings of existing screen readers. In particular, it better handles the use of bit-mapped characters (see Chapter 5). It also has a more consistent set of commands and an extensive help facility. It uses the Dolphin Mimic synthesizer.
Manufacturer Alistair Edwards, University of York
Price Free of charge for non-profit-making use. Requires the Dolphin Mimic synthesizer, which would have to be purchased separately.

Screen Readers for Other Computers

Outspoken See Chapter 5 for a full description.
Manufacturer Berkeley System Design Inc.
Price $395

PS/2 Screen Reader This is a screen reader manufactured by IBM to operate with its PS/2 range of computers. It provides standard screen reader facilities controlled through a special keypad. It can be used with any one of six synthesizers – which is not supplied. It has an extensive programming facility, so that it can be customized to match different applications. It comprises: a control keypad and cable; a floppy disc of software and documentation; three instruction audio cassettes and a printed manual (braille also available).
Manufacturer IBM

Speech Communicators

This section lists both complete communications systems and programs which can be used in conjunction with standard computers and synthesizers to drive them as communicators.

It will be noted from their brief description below that many of the communication programs appear very similar, though developed in different places. This reflects the situation in this area of development: people working in isolation and duplicating one another's efforts. Most developments are started as a response to the specific needs of an individual, in ignorance of what has already been achieved elsewhere.

Claudius Converse This is a speech communicator which allows the user to reproduce pre-stored utterances. Sixty-four utterances are available. Most of them are fixed by the manufacturer, but customers will have some of them customized. For instance, they will have their name inserted in 'This is —— speaking', and their address in 'My address is —— '. Although it can be used for face-to-face communication, its principal use is as a telephone answering machine. The user can listen to the caller and then select appropriate responses in reply. It includes messages which can be used to call for help in an emergency.
Manufacturer British Telecom plc

Control Without Keyboards This is a communication device based on an Apple II, an

Echo synthesizer and a Powerpad membrane keyboard. Various custom layouts of the keyboard can be created and stored. Output can be in either speech or print.
Manufacturer   J Jordan & Associates

Equalizer   See Chapter 4 for a full description of this system.
Manufacturer   Works+ Inc.
UK supplier   Cambridge Adaptive Communications

Fast Access Scan Talker   This program allows an Apple computer with a Cricket or Echo synthesizer to be used as a scanning communication aid. Its vocabulary can be customized. Fast Access Scan Talker has to be used as an enhancement to Speak Up, another Laureate program.
Manufacturer   Laureate Learning Systems Inc.
Price $100

I Can Talk   The user can select by scanning words or symbols from a sixteen-square grid displayed on the computer screen. This program runs on Apple II computers, with either an Echo or Cricket synthesizer. The program also has a teaching mode in which the student must match target phrases.
Manufacturer   Soft Cole
Price $75

Light Talker   See Chapter 4 for a full description.
Manufacturer   Prentke Romich Company
UK supplier   Liberator Ltd
Price   £2,985

Magic Cymbals   This program runs on Apple IIs, with either a Cricket or an Echo synthesizer. It allows the user to select from a set of symbols, through a single-switch scanning system. Words corresponding to the symbols are then spoken.
Manufacturer   Schneier Communication Unit
Price $125

Message Maker   Message Maker is a communicator based on the Apple II computer and Echo or Cricket synthesizer. It can be driven by either a keyboard or a single-switch scanning system. It has a user-definable vocabulary of up to 20,000 characters. Individual messages are composed from word and phrase lists and can be spoken or printed.
Manufacturer   Communication Enhancement Clinic
Price $50–75 (depending on version)

Multi-Scan   This program is based on single-switch scanning. The vocabulary is customizable and the programmer must make corresponding screen overlays. The user can then select from the screen when the appropriate section of the overlay is highlighted. The program runs on Apple II or IBM PC computers and uses a Votrax PSS synthesizer.
Manufacturer   Words+ Inc.
Price $80

Orovox   This is a synthesizer which is controlled by a Concept Keyboard touch-sensitive input pad. It has 248 pre-programmed words and phrases, and capacity for the same number programmed by the user. There are limited facilities to alter the speech pronunciation. It can also be linked to a BBC computer for greater power and flexibility. It may be powered by batteries or mains.

Quick Talk This program works with a number of synthesizers (Echo, Cricket, Votrax PSS and Type 'n' Talk) and runs on Apple II computers. It enables the user to recall selections from its customized vocabulary through three-digit codes.
Manufacturer Schneier Communication Unit
Price $45

RIC Easy Talker This is a program which runs on Apple II computers with a Votrax synthesizer. The user creates messages by selection from menus composed either of alphanumeric characters or words and phrases. Choices are presented in an auditory form. The vocabulary can be customized.
Manufacturer Rehabilitation Institute of Chicago
Price $135

Scan and Speak This communicator is based on an Apple II computer and a Votrax or Echo synthesizer. It allows selection of user-defined phrases through a single-switch input.
Manufacturer Communication Enhancement Clinic
Price $75

Sentence-Scan This communicator is based upon the Apple II range of computers. Up to twenty lists of words can be stored and selected through a keyboard or a single- or dual-switch scanning system. Messages are displayed in large print on the screen, and can be spoken and printed.
Manufacturer Computers to Help People Inc.
Price $15

Simplecom I An Apple II program, designed to teach the communication of daily needs and other early communications skills, based on simple yes/no communication. It requires a Powerpad membrane keyboard and an Echo synthesizer.
Manufacturer Dunamis Inc.
Price $50

Simplecom II Another Apple II program, designed to teach the communication of basic needs. It requires a Powerpad membrane keyboard and an Echo synthesizer. The user can select from symbols displayed on the Powerpad to generate stored phrases. The program comes with ten messages built in and more can be added
Manufacturer Dunamis Inc.
Price $50

Speak Up This program allows an Apple computer with a Cricket or Echo synthesizer to be used as a scanning communication aid. Pre-programmed and customized words may be used. This is the basic version of the program, to which Fast Access Scan Talker can be added as an enhancement.
Manufacturer Laureate Learning Systems Inc.
Price $95

Talk II This is a program for Apple II computers and Echo synthesizers. The user

selects from word, phrase and sentence menus through a scanning mechanism. The vocabulary can be customized by the user and output can be either in speech or print.
Manufacturer G. E. Rushakoff, Clinical Microcomputer Laboratory
Price $90

Talking Bliss Apple This program is based on the Bliss symbolic language and runs on Apple II computers. Using a single switch, keyboard or one of certain compatible communication aids, the user can select, display, speak and print Bliss symbols and messages. The program is compatible with Votrax PSS and Type 'n' Talk synthesizers.
Manufacturer Trace Center
Price $37

Talking Wheelchair This is an Atari-based program which comes with plans for building a complete wheelchair-based communication aid. All selections are made with single keystrokes.
Manufacturer Computers to Help People Inc.
Price $15 for the software, approximately $1,400 to build the complete system

Talking word board This is software which combines Apple II computer, Unicorn Keyboard, Adaptive Firmware Card and Echo speech synthesizer as a talking word board communicator.
Manufacturer Adaptive Peripherals
Price Complimentary

Touch and Speak This communicator is based on an Apple II computer and any one of Echo, Cricket, Votrax or Dectalk. It uses either a standard or a membrane keyboard which defines up to 600 message addresses. Messages are user-definable and can be spelled out as well as spoken whole. Some additional hardware may be required.
Manufacturer Communiation Enhancement Clinic
Price $75

Touch Com This is a training tool for a person who is going to use an electronic communication aid. It runs on Apple II computers with an Additional Powerpad membrane keyboard and Echo synthesizer (not included). The user causes words and phrases to be spoken by pressing different areas of the pad.
Manufacturer Developmental Equipment
Price $128

Touch Talker See Chapter 4 for full description.
Manufacturer Prentke Romich Company
UK supplier Liberator Ltd
Price £2,544

Type and Speak As with Touch and Speak, this is a communicator based on an Apple II computer and any one of Echo, Cricket, Votrax or Dectalk. Messages are typed in letter by letter, spoken once and then erased by the next message. Letters can be input either from a conventional keyboard or through an optional scanning array and switch.
Manufacturer Communication Enhancement Clinic
Price $50

Write An educational program for the Apple II with which the student builds up

sentences from words displayed sequentially on the screen. Output can be either speech or print.
Manufacturer   Computers to Help People Inc.
Price $25

Talking Watches, Clocks and Calculators

Calcu-talk   Calcu-talk is a customized, speech-output version of the Canon CP1211 desk-top print/display calculator. The voice announces the display's contents when the 'talk' button is pressed. It features: a twelve-digit display; an integral colour printer (positive numbers are printed in black, negative in red); eight decimal-place settings and a two-way item counter.
Supplier   Science Products
Price $599

Crystal Talk   This is a fashionably designed cubic talking alarm clock. The time is spoken on the press of a button and it has an LED time and date display.
Supplier   LS & S Group Inc.
Price $75

Falck 5510   This is a calculator with very high-quality, human-sounding speech. A range of voices is available.
Supplier   Falck Produkter A/S

Howard Miller alarm clock   This clock will speak the time at the press of a button and can also be set to announce the time every hour. It has an LCD visual display.
Manufacturer   LS & S Group Inc.
Price $38.95

Satoki talking watch   This watch speaks the time on the press of a button, and also on every hour and half-hour. It also has a visual display of the time and a one-hour timer.
Supplier   Sensory Visionaid
Price   £35

Sharp EL640   This is a speaking calculator, clock and calendar. It includes features for count-up and count-down alarms and time announcements.
Supplier   Visionaid Systems
Price   £69

Sharp talking clock/calculator   This calculator/clock announces the function selected (add, subtract, etc.), entered digits, results, year, month and day. The time is automatically announced every hour. It has an eight-digit LCD visual display, a daily chime alarm and a count-down timer.
Supplier   LS & S Group Inc.
Price $70

Sharp talking clock/radio-cassette   This is an AM/FM stereo radio and cassette player/alarm which will speak the time at the press of a button.
Supplier   LS & S Group Inc.
Price $120

Spartus talking alarm clock   This clock will speak the time at the press of a button and can also be set to announce the time every hour. It has two independent alarm settings and a spoken facility for checking the setting. The volume is adjustable and there is a large LED visual display.
Supplier   LS & S Group Inc.
Price $36

Talking time   Whereas most of the clocks mentioned in this section have been designed with speech as a bit of a gimmick for sighted users, this one was intended for use by blind people and so allows them to set and operate it. It is a pocket-sized clock and has a carrying case. The time is announced when a bar is pressed. It can be set to announce the time on the hour. It has an alarm which can give either a verbal or musical sound and has a count-down timer. The time is also displayed visually in LCD figures.
Supplier   LS & S Group Inc.
Price $30

Talking wrist-watch   The time is announced in hours and minutes and also whether it is a.m. or p.m. There is also a talking alarm feature. It also has a visual, LCD display.
Supplier   Meridian Metier Ltd
Price   £15

Tcalc   Tcalc is a modified version of the Texas Instruments TI66 programmable scientific calculator.
Manufacturer   Dave Jones, Open University
Price   £143

Time-a-message   An alarm clock in which the alarm call is a pre-recorded message. Any message up to 20 seconds can be recorded.
Supplier   LS & S Group Inc.
Price $60

Voxclock   This is a battery-powered speaking alarm clock. The current time is announced on the pressing of a button. It also features a count-down timer.
Supplier   Intertan UK Ltd
Price   £30

Voxwatch   Voxwatch is a speaking watch with a stopwatch feature. The stopwatch announces the elapsed time every five minutes. The time is also shown on a visual digital display.
Supplier   Intertan UK Ltd
Price   £35

Other Speech-Based Devices for Blind Users

Access PC   This is a speech-based computer system. It is based upon a Bondwell PC with 640 kbytes of memory, dual disc drives, a keyboard, a 36-cm colour monitor, a daisy wheel printer, speech synthesizer and speaker. The software includes Artic Vision, which allows application software to be used in a spoken mode. Options allow for enlarged screen characters and braille production ($600 each).

Supplier Arts Computer Products Inc.
Price $3,495

Beckman 310 multimeter This is a multimeter which has been adapted with voice output. Pressing a speech button causes the numbers in the digital display to be spoken. It measures from 0.1 millivolts to 1 kilovolt; currents from 0.001 milliamps to 10 amps, both AC and DC and resistances from 0.1 ohms to 10 megaohms.
Supplier Science Products
Price $649

Braille 'n' Speak Braille 'n' Speak is a pocket-sized computer with braille-based input and speech output. It is programmed as a braille notebook, a clock, a calendar and a telephone dirctory, and has facilities for transcribing braille into print (with the addition of a printer). Input is through a standard-format seven-key braille keyboard and can be keyed as either Grade I or Grade II (contracted) braille. Up to 200 pages of text can be stored, which can be edited and reviewed through its word-processing facilities. It is battery-powered (rechargeable) and measures 10 × 20 × 2.5 cm and weighs 1 kg. It is supplied complete with headset, batteries and a battery charger.
Supplier Sensory Visionaid
Price £895

Braillewriter This is a portable word-processing and communications device for blind users. Input is through a braille-format keyboard and can be in either Grade I or Grade II (contracted) form. Output can be as speech or printed on a built-in printer. Text can be stored either on cassette tape or on a floppy disc. It is powered by rechargeable batteries and is supplied with a waterproof case and earpiece.
Supplier Visionaid Systems
Price: PCO183 £995
PCO283 (with printer) £1,095
PCO184 (with printer and inbuilt cassette) £1,395
PCO 184 (with inbuilt disc drive) £1,995

Digi-voice tool module This is a speech-output device for use in conjunction with digital read-out instruments such as micrometers, callipers and other gauges. A separate connection cable is also required.
Supplier Science Products
Price $520

Eureka Eureka, also known as the braillist's Filofax, is a portable computer with a braille-style keyboard and speech output. Supplied software comprises: note-taker database, word processor, diary, scientific calculator, stopwatch, alarm clock, calendar, telephone directory (with automatic dialling), music composer, thermometer and voltmeter. Hardware includes a built-in disc drive and modem. An optional braille embosser is also available. The Eureka can also be used as a terminal to another computer, either directly or via the modem. Connections are also available for a printer and an external qwerty keyboard.
Supplier Technovision Systems Ltd
Price £1,468

Kurzweil Personal Reader See Chapter 4 for a full description of this device.

Manufacturer   Kurzweil Computer Products
UK supplier   Sight and Sound Technology
Price   Model 10 (hand scanner only) £7,032
          Model 20 (table-top scanner only) £8,500
          Model 30 (both scanners) £9,885

Nomad   Nomad is a portable IBM-compatible lap-top computer with a braille keyboard, speech and 'soft' braille output, dual disc drives and a modem. Text can be input as Grade II (contracted) braille and either stored in that format or translated into expanded text. The synthesizer can speak at an adjustable rate of 50–700 words per minute and pitch and volume are also adjustable. It speaks with good prosody, based on context. File manipulation is controlled through special Cursorpad keys. Included are a standard video port (for connection to a screen), standard input and output ports and connections for a qwerty keyboard.
Manufacturer   Syntha-Voice Computers Inc.
Price $2,295 (Canadian dollars)

Soundtrack   See Chapter 5 for a full description of this system. It is available at low cost for non-commercial research and evalution purposes. It runs on Apple Macintosh computers. It requires the Macintalk software synthesis program, which must be obtained separately.
Manufacturer   Alistair Edwards, University of York
Price   £20

Speakwriter 200   This is a speech-output device to adapt Brother electronic typewriters. It plugs into the printer port. A spoken help facility then allows letter and function keys to be identified. Features include speech for individual keys or words, assistance setting margins and tabs and review of the text by character, line, word or page.
Supplier   Technovision Systems Ltd
Price   £700

Talk-tach   This is a dwell-volt tachometer with voice output for four-, six- and eight-cylinder cars. It is powered by a rechargeable battery and comes complete with a charger and an earphone.
Supplier   Science Products
Price $595

Vincent Workstation   The Vincent Workstation is a microcomputer system designed for use by blind people. It consists of a set of standard hardware (BBC computer, Votrax synthesizer, modified Perkins brailler, printer) connected together and driven by purpose-built talking software (word processor, BASIC language interpreter, etc.). The system is now somewhat outdated but was a very significant development in its time.
Supplier   Sensory Visionaid
Price   From £2,000

Appendix B Addresses of Manufacturers, Distributors and Other Related Organizations

Adaptive Peripherals
4529 Bagley Avenue North
Seattle
Washington
USA
98103
Telephone: (206) 633 2610

American Printing House for the Blind
PO Box 6085
Louisville
Kentucky
USA
40206
Telephone: (502) 895 2405

Apple Computers Inc.
20525 Mariani Avenue
Cupertino
California
USA
95014
Telephone: (408) 996 1010

Apple Developers' Group
Rosebank House
144 Broughton Road
Edinburgh EH7 4LE
Telephone: 031-557 5719

Arts Computer Products Inc.
145 Tremont Street, Suite 407
Boston
Massachusetts
USA
02111

Berkeley System Design
1708 Shattuck Avenue
Berkeley
California
USA
94709
Telephone: (415) 540 5537

British Telecom Action for Disabled Customers
Room B4036
BT Centre
81 Newgate Street
London EC1A 7AJ
Telephone: (0345) 581456

CALL Centre
University of Edinburgh
4 Buccleugh Place
Edinburgh EH8 9JT
Telephone: 031-667 1438

Cambridge Adaptive Communications
24 Fulbrooke Road
Cambridge CB3 9EE
Telephone: (0223) 312194

COMMUNICATION AIDS
  CENTRES

Belfast
Musgrave Park Hospital
Stockman's Lane
Belfast BT9 7JB
Telephone: (0232) 669501, extn 561

Bristol
Frenchay Hospital
Bristol BS16 1LE
Telephone: (0272) 565656, extn 204

Cardiff
Rookwood Hospital
Llandaff Road
Cardiff
South Glamorgan CF5 2YN
Telephone: (0222) 566281, extn 51

Glasgow
Victoria Infirmary
Langside Road
Glasgow G42 9TY
Telephone: 041-649 4545, extn 5579

London
Charing Cross Hospital
Fulham Palace Road
London W6 8RF
Telephone: 081-748 2040, extn 3064

London
Institute of Child Health
The Wolfson Centre
Mecklenburgh Square
London WC1N 2AP
Telephone: 071-837 7618, extn 9

Newcastle upon Tyne
The Dene Centre
Castle Farm Road
Newcastle upon Tyne NE3 1PH
Telephone: 091-284 0480

Sandwell
Boulton Road
West Bromwich
West Midlands B70 8NR
Telephone: 021-553 0908

Truro
Royal Cornwall Hospital
Treliske
Cornwall TR1 3RY
Telephone: (0872) 74242, extn 7184

Communication Enhancement Clinic
Children's Medical Center
300 Longwood Avenue
Boston
Massachusetts
USA
02115
Telephone: (617) 735 6466

Computers to Help People Inc.
1221 West Johnson Street
Madison
Wisconsin
USA
53719
Telephone: (608) 257 5917

Developmental Equipment
981 Winnetka Terrace
Lake Zurich
Illinois
USA
60047
Telephone: (312) 438 3476

Digital Equipment Corporation
146 Main Street
Maynard
Massachusetts
USA
01754-2571
Telephone: (617) 493 6178

DISABLED LIVING CENTRES

Belfast
Musgrave Park Hospital
Stockman's Lane
Belfast BT9 7JB
Telephone: (0232) 669501, extn 565

Birmingham
260 Broad Street
Birmingham B1 2HF
Telephone: 021-643 0980

Edinburgh
Astley Ainslie Hospital
Edinburgh EH2 2HL
Telephone: 031-447 6271, extn 241

Leeds
The William Merrit, St Mary's
  Hospital
Greenhill Road
Armley
Leeds LS12 3QE
Telephone: (0532) 793140

Leicester
Trent Aids Information
76 Clartendon Park Road
Leicester LE2 3AD
Telephone: (0533) 700747

Liverpool
Youens Way
East Prescott Road
Liverpool L14 2EP
Telephone: 051-228 9221

London
Disabled Living Foundation Equipment
  Centre
380–384 Harrow Road
London W9 2HU
Telephone: 071-289 6111

Manchester
Disabled Living Services
Redland House
2 St Chads Street
Cheetham
Manchester M8 8QA
Telephone: 061-832 3678

Newcastle upon Tyne
Newcastle upon Tyne Council for the
  Disabled
The Dane Centre
Castle Farm Road
Newcastle upon Tyne NE3 1PH
Telephone: 091-284 0480

Portsmouth
Prince Albert Road
Eastney
Portsmouth PO4 9HR
Telephone: (0705) 737174

Sheffield
Sheffield Independent Living Centre
108 The Moor
Sheffield S1 4PD
Telephone: (0742) 737025

Southampton
Southampton General Hospital
Tremona Road
Southampton SO9 4XY
Telephone: (0703) 777222, extn 2414
  or 3233

Stockport
St Thomas Hospital
59a Shaw Heath
Stockport SK3 8BL
Telephone: 061-480 7201

Swindon
The Hawthorn Centre
Cricklade Road
Swindon
Wiltshire SN2 1AF
Telephone: (0793) 643966

Dolphin Systems for the Disabled Ltd
PO Box 83
Worcester WR1 2RN
Telephone: (0905) 754577

Dunamis Inc.
3620 Highway 317
Suwanee
Georgia
USA
30174
Telephone: (404) 932 0485

Alistair Edwards
Department of Computer Science
University of York
York YO1 5DD
Telephone: (0904) 432775

Falck Produkter A/S
Postboks 123
Risor
Norway
N-4951

First Byte Inc.
2845 Temple Avenue
Long Beach
California
USA
90806
Telephone: (213) 595 7006

Frank Audiodata
Kriegsstrasse 13–15
Postfach 1161
Oberhausen-Rheinhausen
West Germany
6839

Handicapped Persons Research Unit
Newcastle-upon-Tyne Polytechnic
Newcastle-upon-Tyne
NE7 7TW
Telephone: (091) 235 8211

Dave Jones
Open University
Technology Faculty
Walton Hall
Milton Keynes MK7 6AA
Telephone: (0908) 274066

J. Jordan & Associates
1127 Oxford Court
Neenah
Wisconsin
USA
54456
Telephone: (414) 725 9046

IBM
UK Support Centre for People with
  Disabilities
IBM Warwick
PO Box 31
Birmingham Road
Warwick CV34 5JL
Telephone: (0926) 32525

Intertan UK Ltd
Tandy Centre
Leamore Lane
Walsall
WS2 7PS
Telephone: (0922) 710000

Kurzweil Computer Products
185 Albany Street
Cambridge
Massachusetts
USA
02139
Telephone: (509) 864 4700

Laureate Learning Systems Inc.
110 East Spring Street
Winooski
Vermont
USA
05404
Telephone: (802) 655 4755

Liberator Ltd
Whitegates
Swinstead
Lincs NG33 4PA
Telephone: (047 684) 391

Bill Loughborough
450 Serbastopol Avenue
Santa Rosa
California
USA
95401

LS & S Group Inc.
PO Box 673
Northbrook
Illinois
USA
60065
Telephone: (708) 498 9777

MacSerious
36 Queen Street
Helensburgh G84 9PU
Telephone: (0436) 6971

Meridian Metier Ltd
Unit 1
Lammas Courtyard
Weldon North Industrial Estate
Corby
Northamptonshire NN17 1FZ
Telephone: (0536) 205145

Mountain Computer
360 El Pueblo Road
Scotts Valley
California
USA
95060

National Federation of Access Centres
Hereward College of Further Education
Bramston Crescent
Tile Hill Lane
Coventry CV4 9SW
Telephone: (0203) 461231

Prentke Romich Company
1022 Heyl Road
Wooster
Ohio
USA
44691
Telephone: (216) 262 1984

Rehabilitation Institute of Chicago
Alan J. Brown Center
345 East Superior Street
Chicago
Illinois
USA
60611
Telephone: (312) 908 2556

**G. E. Rushakoff, Clinical
     Microcomputer Laboratory**
Box 3W
Department of Speech
New Mexico State University
Las Cruces
New Mexico
USA
88003
Telephone: (505) 646 2801

RNIB Commercial Training College
Radmoor Rd
Loughborough
Leicestershire LE11 3BS
Telephone: (0509) 611077

Royal National College for the Blind
College Road
Hereford
Worcestershire HR1 1EB
Telephone: (0432) 265725

Schneier Communication Unit
Cerebral Palsy Center
1603 Court Street
Syracuse
New York
USA
13208
Telephone: (315) 455 7591

Science Products
Box A (Berwyn)
Southeastern
Pennsylvania
USA
19399

Sensory Visionaid
Unit 10
Cameron House
12 Castlehaven Road
London NW1 8QU
Telephone: 071-485 4485

Sight and Sound Technology
Quantel House
St James Mill Road
Northampton NN5 5JW
Telephone: (0604) 790969

Skill
The National Bureau for Students with
    Disabilities
336 Brixton Road
London SW9 7AA
Telephone: 071-274 0565/071-737
    7166

Soft Cole
1804 Mississippi
Lawrence
Kansas
USA
66044
Telephone: (913) 842 6085

Speech Plus Inc.
461 North Bernardo Avenue
Mountain View
California
USA
94043
Telephone: (415) 964 7023

STC Mercator
South Denes
Great Yarmouth
Norfolk NR30 3PX
Telephone: (0493) 844911

Street Electronics Corporation
1140 Mark Avenue
Carpinteria
California
USA
93013
Telephone: (805) 565 1612

Syntha-Voice Computers Inc.
40 Ophir Road
Hamilton
Ontario
Canada
L8K 3Z1

Technovision Systems Ltd
4 Hazlewood Road
Northampton NN1 1LN
Telephone: (0604) 239363

Telesensory Systems Inc.
455 North Bernardo Avenue
Mountain View
California
USA
94039-7455
Telephone: (415) 960 0920

Trace Research and Development
    Center
on Communication, Control and
    Computer Access for Handicapped
    Individuals
Waisman Center
University of Wisconsin-Madison
Madison
Wisconsin
USA
53706
Telephone: (608) 262 6966

Votrax Inc.
1394 Rankin Drive
Troy
Michigan
USA
48083
Telephone: (800) 521 1350

Words+ Inc.
1125 Stewart Court, Suite D
Sunnyvale
California
USA
94086
Telephone: (408) 730 9588

Appendix C   The Physics of Sound

Sound is the vibration of air molecules. The source of a sound vibrates, setting the air molecules around it into vibration. These in turn pass on the vibration to other molecules so transmitting the sound. If such vibrating molecules are incident upon an ear, the vibrations are detected and perceived as sounds. Molecules vibrate in a uniform manner which is characterized as a *waveform*. Waves can be produced in a variety of media (water waves in the sea, light waves, etc.) but they all share a number of characteristics which enable us to study and analyse them. The simplest waveform is the sine wave (Figure C.1). It is a very pure sound, which is approximated by the sound of a flute.

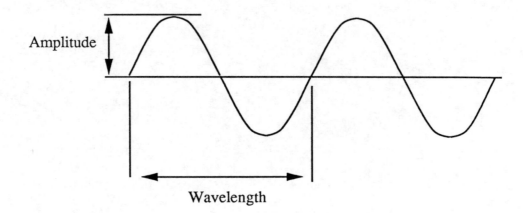

Figure C.1   The simplest form of wave, the sine wave, showing how the amplitude and wavelength are measured

The air molecules are in regular vibration and the rate of vibration, or *frequency*, is very important. Increases in frequency are perceived as increases in the pitch of the sound. Frequency is related to *wavelength*: the shorter a wave, the higher its frequency. In fact there is a simple relation:

Speed = frequency × wavelength

The speed of sound is essentially a constant. If a sound is generated at one position it takes time for the air molecules at another location to be set into vibration, and that time lag represents the speed of the sound. It is of the order of 700 mph, so is not observable over short distances. The loudness of a sound corresponds to its *amplitude*. Frequency is measured in cycles per second, or Hertz (abbreviated to Hz).

Many of the perceptual phenomena of sounds can be explained mathematically. A simple example is the octave. Notes which are an octave apart sound somehow similar. That is to say that a person who is played two notes which are an octave apart is quite likely to say that he or she has heard the same note. The physical explanation is that the frequency of the higher note is exactly twice that of the lower one. For example, the frequency of middle C is 264 Hz, and the C an octave higher has a frequency of 528 Hz.

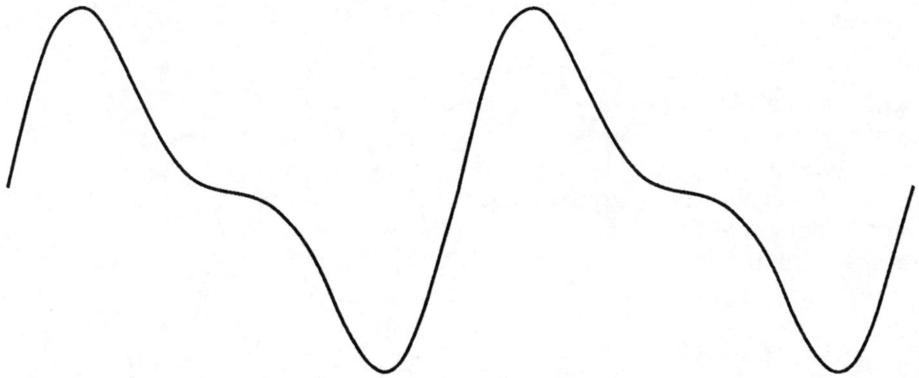

Figure C.2   *A sine wave with an added overtone. This is effectively two waves added together. More complex waveforms (including speech) are essentially composed of a lot more waves summed in this way.*

Most sounds are not as pure as that made by a flute. They are made up of waves of different frequencies, known as *overtones*, superimposed on one another, forming complex sounds. Figure C.2 shows a more complex waveform. The basic sine wave is still discernible, and this is called the *fundamental* of the wave, but added on to it are other waveforms with different amplitudes, but whose frequencies are all multiples of the fundamental. Speech is an example of a sound with an extremely rich set of overtones.

Index